Acclaim for

## *Would it* KILL YOU *to Stop* DOING THAT?

"Even the best behaved among us would benefit from a close reading of investigative humorist Henry Alford's brilliant primer on gracious living…Rather than lecture, the boundlessly charming Alford shows us what good manners look like."
—*Vanity Fair*

"How not to offend in tricky social and business situations (stashing the smart phone is just the beginning), by a writer who's as cheekily charming as he is helpful."
—*O, the Oprah Magazine*

"Wickedly witty…a charming, funny, Noel Cowardesque primer in smartening up."
—*Publishers Weekly* (starred review)

"Consistently fun writing."
—*Newsday*

"He shows himself to be a discreet, keen observer rippling with bad-boy humor. Alford is a razor-wicked, fun guy to be around, and each of his stories are like those 'tiny acts of grace' brightening your day."
—*Kirkus Reviews*

"Breezy…entertaining…[It] amuses as it informs."
—*New York Times Book Review*

"Breezy and entertaining." —*Toronto Star*

"Charming…brings us a kaleidoscope of viewpoints from etiquette authorities, both likely and unlikely… WOULD IT KILL YOU is a delightful puff pastry of an essay. Enjoy." —*Post and Courier* (SC)

"This is a great little book…amusing and often charming…Alford makes us laugh at our collective foibles and etiquette insecurity, and gently encourages us to do more than what common civility requires."
—*Washington Independent Review of Books*

"Alford is a charming writer, who seems able to spin delightful stuff from whatever straw he happens to stumble across, and his rumination on good behavior is no exception." —Salon.com

"If the lack of consideration being bred by our brave new (TMI-fed) world is driving you to less-than-civil acts, it may be time for this guide to modern manners. Alford weds the inspired lunacy of David Sedaris to the philosophic inquiry of 'The Ethicist' column in *The New York Times,* wittily proving that manners are a way of giving others 'a commodity best described by noted speller Aretha Franklin.'" —*Whole Living*

"Alford examines how a society defines manners and sets forth a framework by which to think about them in the 21st century." —*Washington Post*

"Extremely entertaining…Wry and nimble wit…Whatever the ideals may be, most of us can agree decent manners are a good idea. Thanks to this handbook, we stand a better chance of complying." —*BookPage*

"His flair for adding jovial wit to the proceedings offered is evident in every chapter. He has a natural, informative and clever writing talent…provides a reference point from which to learn, a sympathetic voice of reason and an everyday guide for almost any social situation you could possibly imagine." —EdgeNewYork.com

"Wry and witty." —*Newark Star Ledger*

"Warm, funny…The subject is good manners and Alford covers it with a sly wit that finds humor in even the most difficult circumstances. He takes his research seriously…WOULD IT KILL YOU is not only interesting but outright funny. By the book's end you want to meet the author and it comes as no surprise that he volunteers as a NYC 'greeter' for foreign visitors; he's that charming and engaging." —PortlandBookReview.com

"Engaging and thoughtful...The author's keenly written observations on the demise of common courtesy are spot on, written with a measure of both wit and edginess to keep the reader turning pages."

—*Sunday Republican* (CT)

"With Alford as our witty and waggish gentleman-about-town, WOULD IT KILL YOU is less a reference book than a charmingly self-aware compendium of loosely related treatises." —SpectrumCulture.com

"Alford provides a brisk, amusing glimpse into the world of decorum. There's nothing overtly sobering or condescending here, just some darn good writing produced in such a snarky, cheeky way that it's almost impossible to put down once you've decided to take the plunge."

—*Bay Area Reporter* (CA)

"Unique...informative...a fine-tuned wit."

—*Columbian* (WA)

*Would It*
KILL YOU
*to Stop*
DOING THAT?

# Would It
# KILL YOU
 *to Stop*
# DOING THAT?

*A Modern Guide to Manners*

# HENRY ALFORD

**TWELVE**

NEW YORK  BOSTON

Twelve
Hachette Book Group
237 Park Avenue
New York, NY 10017

www.HachetteBookGroup.com

Printed in the United States of America

RRD-C

Originally published in hardcover by Twelve.

First trade edition: February 2013
10  9  8  7  6  5  4  3  2  1

Twelve is an imprint of Grand Central Publishing.
The Twelve name and logo are trademarks of Hachette Book Group, Inc.

The Hachette Speakers Bureau provides a wide range of authors for speaking
events. To find out more, go to www.hachettespeakersbureau.com
or call (866) 376-6591.

The publisher is not responsible for websites (or their content) that are not
owned by the publisher.

The Library of Congress has cataloged the hardcover edition as follows:
Alford, Henry, 1962-
   Would it kill you to stop doing that? : a modern guide to manners /
Henry Alford.
      p. cm.
   Summary: "A laugh-out-loud guide to modern manners"—Provided by the
publisher.
   ISBN 978-0-446-55766-5
   1. Etiquette.  I. Title.
   BJ1853.A39 2012
   395.02'07—dc23

2011036113

ISBN 978-0-446-55765-8 (pbk.)

*Would It*
KILL YOU
*to Stop*
DOING THAT?

## I

*In which the author visits the worldwide epicenter of manners, and has a vexing experience with bananas.*

You need spend only twenty-four hours in my beloved New York City to unearth the city's essential truth: People really know how to spit here. These ain't no dainty, Catherine Deneuve–type loogies we're talkin' about, yo—these are liquid blow darts. This shit'll mess you up.

Also: Looking for a fun little fistfight, or to be casually body-checked? Need compelling evidence that "rabble" does not require more than one rabbler?

We got you covered.

Which is why I'd traveled almost seven thousand miles from my home to Japan.

Japan, the Fort Knox of the World Manners Reserve.

## The Tokyo Lowdown

The best way to get a really good look at something in your day-to-day life is, of course, to not look at it at all. Leave it behind in a pile on the floor. Go somewhere where things are so different, where every one of your preconceptions and assumptions will be made so glaringly obvious, it will be like looking at pictures of yourself naked: searingly verité.

If the thing you want to look at is manners, and the place you go to is Japan, all the better: here is a place where etiquette has been burnished to a high art. To enter these highly codified realms is to be alternately baffled, delighted, aggrieved, wonderstruck.

I had two teachers during my stay in Tokyo. The first was a Japanese etiquette coach I'd hired for a two-hour lesson. A warm, attractive, bespectacled woman in her thirties, Aiko Uda offered cultural immersion classes to individuals and groups in Tokyo; formerly, while living in Canada, she helped hotels and other companies understand the psyches of their Japanese customers.

Aiko had asked me to meet her in a café near the Shinjuku subway station. Her vibe was equal parts friendly and purposeful—family pet meets loan officer.

"What do you notice when you're riding on the subway?" Aiko asked me early on in our session.

"No one eats," I suggested.

"Right. No eating or drinking. And a lot of text messaging but no phone calls." She added, "There's so much social pressure here. If someone talked on a phone, people would stare, and that would be a big deal. It's a lot more like a collective here."

Trying not to let Aiko see me, I casually brushed a piece of my green tea muffin into a napkin in an effort at crumb management.

Aiko smiled warmly and then proceeded to run the Japanese manners gauntlet for me.

Slippers: Take your shoes off at the entrance to apartments and any building where others are doing so. Wear slippers on the intermediary flooring, and wear only socks on the tatami. Don't wear the bathroom slippers anywhere but the bathroom, even if they are more "you" than the slippers offered you on arrival.

Pointing: Don't point with your fingers or feet like an orangutan. If you must indicate something, use your palm.

Eye contact: Too much direct eye contact will freak out your interlocutors. Lose the beadiness, my friend.

Doing business in Japan: Be punctual. Wear a dark, conservative suit. Bring a wrapped gift from a department store's food court; spend about ten to twenty thousand yen, and present it with a lot of self-effacing remarks about the gift's modesty. Have a lot of business cards to hand out. Try to hand out and receive the business cards with both of your hands. Put others' business cards faceup in front of you on a desk or table so you can refer to them. Take notes—it's considered respectful and not wonkish.

The loveliest piece of instruction Aiko offered started with her observation, "We also have this idea of saving face. From the collective. Not to embarrass someone." So when someone mispronounces a word or is unaccountably ignorant of the correct word or term to be used in a conversation, Japanese people will often—instead of outright correcting the person—gracefully interject the correct word into their response. If a visitor to Japan marvels at having flown over a very large mountain that bore an exceptional resemblance to a flattened snow cone, his polite Japanese interlocutor knows to seamlessly drop "Mount Fuji" or "Fuji-san" into his response. Calamitous embarrassment: neatly dodged.

Aiko wondered if I had any questions.

"I read that it's considered impolite to sneeze in public," I said.

"Sneezing is a dirty thing to do. If you can get out of that situation, you should."

"Okay," I said, my mind conjuring the image of a sneeze-threatened salaryman hurriedly getting up from a conference table during a meeting and then plunging out a skyscraper's window.

"If you must, you must. Do it into a napkin that is disposable."

"Got it."

I also had a noodle question.

I'd read in various books that the Japanese audibly slurp their ramen or soba noodles; indeed, two days earlier, my boyfriend, Greg, and I had gone to a mom-and-pop lunch counter to eat terrific bowls of ramen with sliced pork. Unhabituated to slurping as we are, we hadn't made any noise, and I'd wondered if the mom and pop had been a little disappointed in us.

I asked Aiko, "Is it rude *not* to slurp noodles?"

"They would make an exception for you. You are a foreigner and you look like a foreigner."

"We were the only Westerners in this noodle bar. The slurping: It was a wall of sound."

"Maybe sometimes people would look at you—the same as if Japanese people used a knife and fork to eat french-fried potatoes."

I've eaten french fries with a knife and fork before: very nice.

My other etiquette coach in Tokyo was self-elected. Greg and I had walked around Tokyo's bustling wholesale fish market, Tsukiji, one day, and stopped to have sushi at one of the tiny, ramshackle restaurants located near the fish-selling. I'd already learned a lot of restaurant etiquette from books and from Aiko: Don't wipe your face with the hot towel. Use the top ends, not the licked ends, of your chopsticks to take food from a common dish. Hold the rice bowl up close to your mouth, to avoid spilling. Pour sake for others, and let others pour sake for you, but never pour for yourself.

But it was J.J., our waiter at the restaurant at Tsukiji, who gave me the gift of "please." About five feet tall and in his forties, J.J. wore a down vest, designer sunglasses that rested over his ski cap, and a tool belt that dripped with key chains on thin straps of leather; the look was very Gay Ski-Lift Operator.

Typically, I like a waiter or waitress who will flirt with me a tiny bit, just so I know I'm still in the game, but J.J.'s client comportment was less romance than car wash. Emitting a constant stream of excited chattering in his high-pitched nasal voice, he became a blur of suggestions and salutations, an affection dervish.

And then there were the mimeographs that he handed out—jumbled, handwritten concatenations of text featuring phrases and dining instructions in English. Prominently featured on them was the phrase *onegai shimasu* (own-uh-guy shi-MOZ-zoo).

J.J. told me, "You can say 'Sashimi, onegai shimasu.' At end of meal, 'Check. Onegai shimasu.'"

I nodded and then *onegai-shimasu*-ed him.

J.J. returned mid-meal to scribble some phrases and suggestions on the mimeograph. At one point, he started yelling at me "Double hand! Double hand!" and I realized that he wanted me to bring my rice bowl up to my mouth so I would spill less.

A few days after our first visit, I returned to J.J.'s restaurant, without Greg. This time J.J. handed me a *second* mimeograph detailing dining etiquette.

"Why do you do this?" I asked him. "Is it because foreigners have such bad manners?"

J.J. laughed. "It might be!"

## [Sound of Gong]

The Japanese word for "yes" (*hai!*) sounds very, very similar to one of the English words for "hello" (*hi!*). To an unsophisticated linguist such as myself, this is highly confusing, giving the impression of an advanced greeting disorder:

"Excuse me, sir, can you please tell me where the Shibuya subway stop is?"

"Hello! It's down the street, take a left."

"Thank you. So I take a left out your door, then another left?"

"Hello! Hello!"

"*Arigato.* And the Ginza subway line stops at Shibuya?"

"Hello! Hello!"

Feeling unnerved at the beginning of my three-week

stay, I was determined to equip myself with some courtesy words in order to mask my paralysis. At bare minimum—which, sadly, is mostly where I live—the two most important phrases for traveling foreigners to learn, it has always struck me, are "Thank you" and "Excuse me." (Sure, "please" would be a nice thing to have, but in a pinch you can use "Thank you.") "That was delicious" would also be lovely—but it, too, is implied with a very effusive "Thank you." Additionally, "Hello" and "Good-bye" are fine things to know; however, these are both expressions that others will be saying to you a lot, and thus you can simply go into parrot mode. If your mind is as cluttered as mine is, you'll want to keep things to a bare minimum, which brings us back to two pillars of courtesy, "Thank you" and "Excuse me."

Japan-wise, "Thank you very much" was easy—the phrase "*Domo arigato*, Mr. Roboto" echoes in one's head. I found "Excuse me" in my guidebook: *sumimasen* (soo-me-moss-SEN). But as soon as Greg and I had arrived at the airport for our flight to Tokyo, I realized that I wasn't sure if *sumimasen* meant "I'm sorry" as well as "Excuse me." And so I found myself chatting up our Continental Airlines service representative. I'd fallen deeply in love with her even before we started talking: She'd seen me tangling with an obstreperous check-in machine, and had saved me. That her name tag bore the name HIROKO WOODCOCK only sweetened my admiration for this celestial being: a huge head on top of a tiny body, emitting a pleasing stream of guidance and high-pitched murmuring. Think warm, sympathetic eyes. Think neck scarf knotted at throat to resemble silk croissant.

"Hey, I've got a question for you," I added. "If I bump into someone on the street in Tokyo, do I say *sumimasen*?"

"*Sumimasen*, yes."

"I'm trying to be a cultural ambassador."

"You're going to change the world!"

"Yes."

"Like Michael Jackson!"

"Uh, okay."

She paused before counseling, "In Tokyo not many people will say this. They're in a hurry."

"Right."

"But I wish you good luck!"

## Surfing the Wave

Culture clash can be unpretty. Some years ago, singer and actress Diana Ross went to Kenya to "find her tribe." According to *New York* magazine, Ross did a lot of research before arriving at Samatian Island in the middle of Lake Baringo, where she was to meet the ethnic group called the Pokot. All went well until the grandmother of the Pokot's most powerful chief greeted Ross respectfully by "sharing water" with her—i.e., she spat in Ross's face.

Whereupon Ross, bewildered, screamed, "This is *not* my tribe!"

I neatly dodged face spitting in Japan; that said, I knew right away I was very distant from New York City: For two mornings in a row, a construction worker near our hotel bowed at Greg and me as we walked past.

"I hope he's doing that for us and for no one else," I said.

We stopped and stared, heartbroken, as the worker proceeded to bow his head for each passerby.

We wondered how long it would take for the building to be built.

That afternoon, we encountered another example of this intense commitment to decorum. After blithely paying our lunch bill at a restaurant—there's no tipping for services in Japan—we'd walked about a block away when we heard someone running after us and calling out to us: our waitress. She was bearing the ten yen (roughly, eleven cents) that we'd absentmindedly left on our table.

One rainy night, unable to find a restaurant in the Ginza district called Bird Land, I ducked into a shoe store and asked a salesman if he knew of it. "One minute, please," he said, disappearing into a back room to get an umbrella. Umbrella in hand, he motioned me to follow him out of the store where we walked two blocks in the rain, then took a left, walked another block, then ducked down into a subway entrance, went through a door, and turned left again. Motioning with his hand, the salesman said to me, "That is the restaurant." I was gob-smacked. My expression of baffled gratitude, combined with my frenzy of bowing and *domo-arigato*-ing, was nothing short of aerobic.

But no aspect of Japanese culture is as intensely gracious as the opening of department stores every morning. At the beginning of each business day, the sales staff at all of the big Japanese department stores engages in a bowing ritual for the store's customers that lasts about five minutes. Each employee stands in front of his or her counter, creating rows of ten or fifteen bodies down a corridor of a store. They then proceed to bow about forty-five degrees as each customer walks by.

Seldom have I felt more honored. As you walk down a couple hundred feet of cosmetics counters at an old-guard store like Mitsukoshi, your movement sets off a ripple of appreciation that starts directly in front of you, then shimmers briefly over the Lancôme counter prior to wafting up to the ceiling and bursting in a cirrocumulus pillow of good tidings; it's a non-stadium version of "the Wave," and you get to surf it.

I kept returning to department stores during our trip, thinking that the charm of the bowing ritual might fade, but it didn't. Some mornings, thanks to the various stores' staggered opening hours, I could get in *two* openings—say, the Takashimaya store in Nihonbashi at ten o'clock, followed by the Matsuzakaya's opening in Ginza at ten thirty. Waltzing into these stores' embraces and setting off a bodily ripple of good vibes, I felt at once welcomed, acknowledged, loved. Only personalized skywriting would have been more vivid.

## Fruit and Its Implications

All this graciousness does not exist in isolation, however. If the key word for the Japanese mind-set I've alluded to is *adherence*, this adherence can cut both ways. Consider the conversation I had with a Tokyo cabdriver one night. When he broached the topic of how much magazine writers and book authors get paid, I delicately steered the conversation away. He brought it up again, glancingly; I glancingly skittered away. Then he asked me outright how much money I make a year. Here, the energy and sense of mission that in other circumstances might be directed at an elaborate bowing ritual was instead directed at a series of questions you'd expect to hear from your accountant.

Or consider my banana episode. One night, in a grocery store near my hotel in Ueno, I saw some delicious-looking bananas for sale. But because they came in bunches of twelve or fifteen, I snapped four off a bunch. I took them to the cash register.

A faint look of horror passed over the face of the cashier, a skinny, fastidious guy in his thirties. He pointed at the fruit and asked me something in Japanese.

I pantomimed snapping the four bananas off from the larger bunch.

"No. Cannot. Sorry," he said, shaking his head with what seemed more vehemence than necessary.

"*Sumimasen*," I apologized.

He got the attention of his fellow cashier. *Look what the round-eye has done. He has attempted to assert an alien system of portion control.*

The other cashier shook his head, too, and started talking excitedly. *The cheek! Americans: always defiling time-honored and traditional banana configurations!*

I assumed that the next moment in this chain of events would see my cashier either prorating my bananas, or asking me if I wanted to buy a larger bunch.

No.

Instead, he stowed the four pieces of fruit on a shelf near his register for safekeeping. *Bastard bananas. Bananas conceived out of wedlock. Banana untouchables.*

I happened to have a rubber band in my pocket at the time. And so, producing it, I pointed first at my bananas and then at the bunches for sale, and pantomimed a tying motion.

"Not necessary," the cashier said. Pointing at the eight bananas from which I had so brutishly severed the four, he added, "We will make the price of other bananas lower."

And, presumably, incinerate my four bananas in a cleansing ritual at dawn.

## If You Can Get Out of That Situation, You Should

The dark side of *adherence* is perhaps most strongly felt in the presence of crowds. Anyone who has visited a shrine in Japan and found himself amid a sea of grandmothers knows whereof I speak. These tiny wonders, all built to two-thirds scale, push inexorably toward the basin into which people are throwing good-luck coins, as if possessed. You'd sooner lie down in front of a tank than these grannies. They will thresh you.

More famously, the Tokyo subway testifies to the thesis that the Japanese mob is a powerful mob. In *Underground*, novelist Haruki Murakami's non-fiction account of the 1995 Sarin gas attacks, one subway rider tells of getting on a crowded subway car with his briefcase. When his briefcase gets caught between two other passengers who are moving forward in the mass of bodies, the rider is forced to choose: let go of his briefcase or break his arm.

## Where You Go

Though J.J., Aiko, and the woman behind the desk at our hotel were wonderful fonts of information, there was one bit of Japanese etiquette that I felt uncomfortable broaching with them. This, of course, was the topic of perilous Japanese toilets. These bad boys, as you probably know, often come equipped with a console arm that is loaded down with buttons—one to summon a bidet feature, one to create flushing sounds (to mask embarrassing sounds), a seat warmer, an air dryer. The Japanese toilet, in short, is one-stop shopping.

One night, upon entering the single-toilet men's room of a restaurant, I was slightly surprised to be greeted there by the toilet's seat automatically lifting itself up. *Hello/hai!* Fortunately, I had to pee. I did so, and then left the bathroom, the seat still up. As I left the bathroom, I thought, Surely I wasn't meant to lower the seat myself, either manually or by button? Or was I? That the restaurant was fairly crowded with diners only heightened my anxiety and potential humiliation. I imagined a CEO in a three-piece suit entering the bathroom and being thrown into moral crisis…Or a restaurant employee forced to cleanse the bathroom of my transgression via some elaborate ceremony featuring incense and flashing swords… *Banana ritual at dawn.*

So I devised a game plan: Walk out of bathroom, close door, stand in front of door, and wait fifteen seconds to see if seat goes down again; if anyone should see me closing door and waiting in front of it, I'd quickly reenter bathroom pretending to have dropped wallet or important legal document.

I closed the door and waited; no men in need showed up. When I reentered the bathroom, the seat was still up. Meanwhile, the toilet clicked and thrummed in a state of almost military readiness; it sounded like it was about to produce small feet, walk out of the bathroom, and get on with its day.

I looked at the console arm and saw a series of illustrations—a spray of water; some squiggly, vaporous lines; and something that looked like an occluded front on a TV weather map. I started to reach out to touch one of the buttons when a small voice inside my head said, *No. Don't do a Diana.*

Jittery, I returned to my table, where I would describe my facial expression as "darty-eyed."


## I Can't Thank You Enough

On the last day of my twenty days in Tokyo, I returned to J.J.'s restaurant. He automatically reached for one of his mimeographs to present me, and I removed my hat and said, "*Konnichiwa.* It's me." He smiled in recognition.

I said, "I've been eating in Japan for a couple of weeks now, so my manners should be much better."

"Yes! Very good!"

I ordered the sashimi, as I had the last time I'd eaten there, largely because it contained the best thing I would eat in Japan: a sweet, raw scallop the size of a child's kneecap.

A few nights prior, I'd told the receptionist at my hotel about the shoe salesman who had walked three blocks in the rain with me to show me where the restaurant Bird Land was, and had told her that I wished I'd known a more exalted phrase than *domo arigato* to offer him. She'd taught me *tazukah di moshita*, which translates literally as "You saved my life."

So, seated at the counter of J.J.'s restaurant having finished my child's kneecap and other raw offerings, I told him, "*Tazukah di moshita*."

His eyes popped wide open, Twinkle City.

"Very nice!" he trilled.

Realizing that the next step in my departure would be for me to stand and initiate the frenzy of bowing that most Japanese social occasions end with, I decided first to warn him.

"J.J., I hurt my back walking all over the city yesterday."

"Yes?"

He cocked his head, uncertain in the face of this terribly fascinating information.

"So when I stand up to go," I explained, "I'm just going to do one tiny head bow, even though you deserve a lot more."

He frowned exaggeratedly, and I wondered if I'd overstepped some boundary. But then he offered, "Okay, I understand."

As I bowed, I realized that I wanted my bow to contain everything I had learned and come to love about Japan and its culture.

It almost did.

## II

*In which the author defines his terms
regarding the topic at hand, puts forth a
theory based on an appliance not typically
associated with same topic, and then
tries to part some clouds labeled
"Received Wisdom."*

I take my manners for granted. Like you, I imagine, I have some lovely ones and I have some slightly less lovely ones. (Okay, let's be honest: I have some truly appalling ones.) But on the whole, I assume that I am, both to my circle of familiars and to people unknown to me, mostly inoffensive, intermittently cheery, and occasionally even elf-like.

As it turns out, however, everyone else in the world takes *his* manners for granted, too—and thinks he's mostly operating in the clear. So who left that thirty-year-old Dorito-encrusted sofa out on the sidewalk where it's blocking traffic? It's been hemorrhaging loose change like a Tilt-A-Whirl.

My investigation into manners got its kick start when I read one day that Edmund Burke, the eighteenth-century Irish writer and philosopher, said that manners are more important than laws. Thinking it over, I realized that I wholly agree. At the end of each day, my life has been far more affected by the small indignities, or the tiny acts of grace, than by any piece of governmental legislation. Anxiety over a slight or insult that I've absent-mindedly delivered is percolating in my brain—as is the fact that a colleague hasn't returned my e-mail in nine days (and I'm not even going to mention the stranger who clipped his toenails in my proximity a week ago, even though I am haunted daily by the severed nails' screams of terror as they sailed through the air). By contrast, the fact that I can't sell my apartment without reporting it, or carry a firearm, or buy marijuana legally occupies a much more remote part of my psyche. And though my unreturned e-mail and my slight to a friend seem, in their normalcy and their insularity, to be tiny, they are in fact huge to me.

There are times in life when you notice the world's ills, and sigh in contemplative resignation; and there are times when you notice the world's ills, and grab a pair of rubber gloves and a bottle of Windex. In my case, the quotidian and everyday nature of the issues at hand made me think I might stand a chance of tackling them. I mean, it wasn't like I needed to be a Martin Luther

King or an Erin Brockovich here—I am Unreturned E-Mail Man, hear me roar; I am Clipped Toenails Survivor, avast ye!

In light of this, I decided to study these tiny-but-huge things: to read about them, and travel in their name, and talk to experts like Miss Manners and Tim Gunn and a former member of a street gang. I wanted to volunteer myself as an online etiquette coach for some of my colleagues and friends. I wanted to train my eyes on the world's most terrifying bride. I wanted to know the ways in which I unknowingly offend others. I wanted to pierce the mantle of obliviousness that overcomes me whenever I enter a restaurant and play a game called "Touch the Waiter."

I wanted, in short, to hold up a magnifying glass to unattractive habits that I stumble upon, be they my own or others'.

I hope that we're still talking by the end of the book.


## Up to the Point of Crime or Bodily Harm

We all know bad manners when we see them. For some, an airborne accumulation of spit would incontrovertibly constitute bad manners; for others, it might be a sneeze in public.

But what exactly are good manners? I'd like to think

I have them, but anecdotal evidence sometimes suggests otherwise.

For that matter, what is it to have manners at all? We have heard it said of so-and-so that "he has no manners!" We understand what that means, but just what is it he has none of?

It's easier to say what bad manners are: any action that makes you feel stupider or slower or more like a wet-lipped monkey than you actually are. Especially when you're the offender's peer or loved one. Being asked how much money you earn. Having your car barricaded into its parking space by a driver who's apparently reciting the closing chapters of *War and Peace* to a bystander. Standing in line behind the customer who, post-purchase, has colonized the stretch of counter next to the cash register as Her Own Little Deskspace. Hearing the words "Nice to meet you" from someone with whom you recently spent seven meaningful hours. Being told—no, chided—that little Dylan cannot eat peanuts so could you please please please make sure that the sleeping bag you're lending him was not manufactured in a county that has a nut-processing plant.

But crystallizing "good manners" is a more challenging task. If we provisionally define *manners* as "how we treat one another, short of matters of crime or bodily harm"—crime or bodily harm being the point at which manners vault into ethics—then good manners means treating one another well.

It's also essential not just to define manners, but to differentiate between manners and their close cousins. For instance, while the two are often blurred, manners and style are two different things. Manners involve interaction: someone's actions affecting another person. Style, by comparison, does not. The PhD without medical accreditation who calls himself "Dr." may seem a bit insecure, but he is not committing a manners violation—that is, until he requires *others* to refer to and address him as "Dr." At this point, his unfortunate style crosses the line into manners, and becomes a broader concern.

Manners also imply expectation. If your friend likes to paint mist-enshrouded pictures of world leaders' heads grafted onto kitty cats' bodies, this is, in and of itself, unrelated to manners. But as soon as she gives you one of these paintings, framed, as a present, and insinuates that it would look great above your mantelpiece, then she enters into the arena of bad manners because her act throbs with expectation.

Most of us seem to use the words *manners*, *etiquette*, and *protocol* interchangeably, so perhaps it makes sense to clarify here, too, lest confusion reign. As I see it, manners are principles, and etiquette is the specific acts of these principles. Protocol is a subset of etiquette, being the etiquette of a particular milieu. To get all metaphorical on you: Manners are a general geography of behavior; etiquette is a mountain within that geography; protocol is the wash from the mountain stream that's threatening to turn your backyard into a silty hellpit.

~⊙~

What makes all this definition and differentiation tricky is that tone often trumps action—it's all, to paraphrase Noël Coward, a question of lighting. A statement uttered by a charming person who's smiling, as opposed to a severe person who's barking, can have different meanings. "I didn't know that!" as a reaction to the announcement of someone's pregnancy is, when accompanied by foot stomping and excitement, palpable evidence of the couple's joy spreading to others; but if accompanied by cinched lips and an ominous stare, it's another story altogether.

Sometimes we're given cues to a situation's tone or context by non-vocal means, too: Larry David has said he chose the bouncing, Fellini-esque theme music for *Curb Your Enthusiasm*, his take on modern manners, because, "You can really act like an imbecile and this music is going to make it okay." The words "Festive Attire" on an invitation are a sign that your Hawaiian shirt collection need go uncelebrated no longer; the sight of other fiber artisans busily clicking their needles and paying out wool during the PTA meeting means it's probably okay for you, too, to unveil that part of your personality that your less tolerant friends call Yarnivore.

Manners, as most of these examples illustrate, are

relative. They probably always have been; but in a post-Einsteinian world, it's truer than ever. In days of yore, when roughly 99 percent of all human beings never interacted with others outside the context of a village inhabited by what was effectively their own tribe, manners could afford to be a lot more absolute, a lot less context-, situation-, and place-and-time-specific. The first public coach service in England appeared in 1637; as the English became mobile and started interacting regularly with foreigners, a whole new legal system, called piepowder law, had to be instituted to deal with the problems that arose when people of different ranks and nationalities started to intermingle.

Our country's shift from an industrial nation to a service economy has bolstered the current and pressing need for more civil conduct, too: He who once used a big piece of metal to form and shape lots of smaller pieces of metal now wears an aqua vest and a name tag that reads ASSISTANT MANAGER. With this aqua vest come a raft of new responsibilities, many of them involving meetings and negotiations and regional sales reps and Frequent Buyer cardholders—a million opportunities, in short, to foster misunderstanding and interpersonal mayhem.

But surely there are universal principles to be found here; a manners equivalent to a mathematical constant, or a unified field theory of manners? Some global, always-appropriate commonalities that link certain actions and place them safely under the umbrella of good manners?

I certainly hope so. I'd like to think that being modest about one's achievements, taking a newcomer in hand and explaining some of the peculiarities of a new setting to him, are both considered thoughtful acts around the world.

And I'd also like to think I can enter any given cultural context—the Navajo, the Lapp, suburban Arkansas Bible thumpers, a Shanghai Triad—and, despite obvious sartorial and lingual handicaps, create a good-enough impression that one gangster or born-again would turn to another and say, "Oh, you'll like Henry—" And then add, after a pause for dramatic import, "He's not a *complete* asshole."

## Inheriting the Toilet Seat

If my sojourn to Japan taught me anything, it was that human relations are sort of like bathrooms: We are perpetually inheriting the toilet seat. Every time we emerge from a single-stall facility, we are responsible for the state of that facility's toilet seat, regardless of whether anyone is standing outside and glaring at us as we slink forth. Even if the only reason we were in the bathroom was to fuss over our problematic new haircut, should we not grab a paper towel and do a quick wipe-off of the seat? (One can, of course, bring style to bear on this operation—I have been known, if only to myself, to unravel an oven-mitt-size accumulation of toilet paper; to place it gingerly on the toilet's seat; and to use my right foot to guide this oven mitt over the problem area.) Who wants to run the risk of being thought of as a splasher?

I subscribe to the theory that we are all constantly rewriting or adding to the definition of various words and phrases and things and actions. Life is a cosmic Wikipedia. If you are a CPA who cooks his books, then you are defining a CPA as "someone who sometimes cooks the books." If you're a mother of three who loves PBS and the Discovery Channel, then you're saying to the world that mothers are "women who love extreme close-ups of insects." To the global conception of what a CPA or a mother is, you are adding precedents and details about creative accounting and thickly furred antennae.

And so, too, with toilet seats and humanity. We are, all of us, every day, adding to the Wikipedia entry for *humanity*.

We are, all of us, eternally, inheriting and bequeathing the toilet seat.

## Quills, One of Them Samuel Johnson's

*Wipe off the toilet seat even if I haven't used it?*, I hear you gasp, your eyes unfocused and shifty, as if in the presence of nuclear weaponry or house-sized lizards. *Did I just spend twenty-four dollars to have someone encourage me to be a restroom attendant?*

I admit it: This is more effort than anyone likes to make. Moreover, it feels somewhat...gross. And don't get me started about the germs—I'd sooner lick most sidewalks than touch all but the most exalted of toilet seats.

But hear me out: Good manners don't come naturally. They do not exist in a vacuum. They are—for most of us, anyway—artificial: a construct. They are what Samuel Johnson characterized as "fictitious benevolence." Worse, they require constant calibration.

An old German folktale tells the story of a group of porcupines who live in an area so cold, they will freeze when they stand too far apart from one another, but succumb to impalement if they stand too close. Settling at last on a state of mutually inconvenient cooperation, they call their artificial state good manners.

Indeed, only by practicing good manners can we proceed unkebabbed.

I'd like to turn your attention to some of the misconceptions surrounding manners. Like one of those pieces of yellowed, sticky flypaper that you find twisting from the ceiling of a gas station on the highway, the concept of manners is thick with carcasses. Flies are sticking to other flies. Encrustment in session.

In twenty-first-century America, the prevailing ethos for social interaction is "Do what makes you feel

comfortable." The problem with such an approach is that
*comfortable*, if left up to most of us, is not a pretty picture. I'd be entirely comfortable, frankly, skipping your
piano recital in favor of lying on my couch in my underpants, idly flipping through the current issue of British
*GQ*. And you'd probably be most comfortable if, at gatherings, you could walk behind the bar and fix your own
goddamn martini, thank you. That's just how we are.
Couple of charmers.

But the world deserves more from us. From all 6.9 bil-
lion of us. It's not comfortable for me to walk up to, and
start to talk to, the person at a party who's standing alone
and staring at the floor; I'd rather stand here talking to
this oddly attractive person who's just told me he read my
last book. Nor is it particularly comfortable to ask your
neighbor whether your music is too loud when you put
your speakers out on the patio, or to ask your wheelchair-
bound co-worker whether you might be the designated
car parker in his handicapped space on the day he's supposed to be off.

But to do these things—these things that may lie outside our comfort zones—is to be a good porcupine.

Studies show that we're less likely to be rude to people
we know well; so all this porcupine business needs special attention when our fellow quill owners are not our
familiars.

Indeed, the story of manners is to a large degree the
story of strangers. During the first two decades of the

nineteenth century, America saw an upsurge in interest in manners; social historians link this to the rise of the industrial city. Sure, most of the people who bought etiquette manuals were interested in upward mobility, in bettering their financial or social lot. But coiled within this highly practical impulse is a more philosophical one, too. Living with others, regardless of whether we know them or not, asks us to suspend a part of ourselves—to hold some of our impulses in abeyance, to curb our throbbing id. But people who move to densely populated areas have to do all this suspending (a) more frequently and (b) despite the fact that they don't know any of the people they're interacting with, and probably never will.

In today's world this dynamic remains, but for different reasons. Today we immigrate and emigrate and outsource and vacation at the drop of a hat. Strangers is where we live.

## "R-E-S-P-..."

Many people are resistant to the cultivation of—if not the very mention of—etiquette; they decry its air of elitism, its self-importance, its effete white gloves. But I would argue that in truth, the *elitist* thing to do is to denounce manners. To suggest that we don't need to practice good manners is to ignore the differences that exist among us, and to suggest that these differences are nothing more than misunderstandings or miscommunications—things that will disappear if we simply proceed along the path of least resistance. As Judith Martin, aka Miss Manners, wrote in the fittingly modest masterpiece *Common Courtesy*, "The rationale that etiquette should be eschewed because it fosters inequality does not ring true in a society that openly admits to a feverish interest in the comparative status-conveying qualities of sneakers."

When I suggest that we are all different, I don't simply mean that Nasar, a devout Muslim, hails from a farming community in which it has not rained in living memory, while Beverly, blind, is a little handsy, while Sean grew up orphaned and homeless on the streets of Mexico City, while Edwig, Danish royalty, is impervious to nuance. I mean that even within groups of people with highly similar backgrounds, we will still encounter huge variations. For instance, among my peer group of white, college-educated, left-leaning writers and editors who grew up middle class in the suburbs and now work in the arts or media and live in New York City—a rather limited demographic—I find widely varying attitudes about answering cell phones during meals; asking questions about income, expenditures, careers, and sex; talking about the parties or functions that your mutual friends threw, but that you weren't invited to; making introductions; writing thank-you notes; and apologizing.

There's a metaphor to be made here about snowflakes, but I've already saddled you with the porcupines and the public toilets, and this whole thing is in danger of turning into a Grand Canyon–themed snow globe. So I'll just speak simply about what makes me think we could all profit from a frank discussion of how we all behave. Americans have an essential conflict with manners. We yearn for the predictability and sense of order that manners provide, but we are turned off by the elitism and privilege that they seem to bespeak. But the fact is, manners don't need to take the form of asparagus forks and "My good sir"; the manners I'm talking are available to all regardless of station in life. Contrary to popular opinion, manners are not a luxury good that's interesting only to those who can afford to think about them. The essence of good manners is not exclusivity, nor exclusion of any kind, but sensitivity. To practice good manners is to confer upon others not just consideration but esteem; it's to bathe others in a commodity best described by noted speller Aretha Franklin.

I interviewed Judith Martin, Miss Manners, for this book, and one of the things she told me speaks volumes about the non-elitism of good manners in America. For our meeting, Martin had asked me to pick a location anywhere in her Washington, DC, neighborhood—"People always ask me why I don't give interviews in my home," she said. "I tell them, 'Because I live there.'" So I had invited her to come sit in my hotel's lobby. With her unaffected warmth, brown tweed suit, and large up-swoop of white hair, Martin instantly put me in mind of a favorite art history teacher; we sat and sipped tea and gabbed in the manner of a noted medievalist and her Thursday-evening TA.

Martin explained to me one of the sources of Southern hospitality, which will surprise some. "In pre–Civil War, so-called Southern aristocracy, a lot of these people came from very humble origins and turned land into money, and began to fancy that they were English country gentlemen and ladies. But who taught manners to their children? The slaves. The *household* slaves. The household slaves tended to be from the upper class of their tribes, and they had a high sense of hospitality and deference, which they taught to these little Southern children. This open hospitality—'Y'all come,' and using a first name with an honorific like 'Miss May,' and calling people uncle or aunt when they're not related—a lot of these customs can be traced back to the slaves because the lady of the house was just fanning herself and turning the children over to Mammy."

"And when you tell this to Southerners," I asked, "what kind of reaction do you get?"

"Some are very pleased," she said. "Others not."

Wealth and milieu are untrustworthy indexes of the importance people attach to manners. When I say to you "highly codified behavior based on a cutthroat adherence to hierarchical status," you might suppose I'm talking about an Edith Wharton novel, but in fact I'm talking about prison. Prior to rehabilitating himself and writing a series of books aimed at empowering street youth, Randy Kearse was a bit of a badass. As head of a multi-state crew with over forty workers, moving more than fifty kilos of crack cocaine during one two-year period, he did well for himself and his organization—and for his trouble spent thirteen years in prison. He makes federal prison and life in a two-man cell sound like it requires NASA training. He told me: "You have a sink in the cell. But you do not spit in the sink. Everyone in prison is a germophobe. You spit in the toilet. You do not spit in the sink. You do not go to the bathroom while your cellmate is in the cell. To notify him that you're using the toilet while he's out of the cell, you put a towel over the glass part of the cell. In the chow room, when you're eating and one of you is done, but others are still eating, you knock twice on the table before leaving. I have no idea why. It's done in every prison. It's like a kid asking permission to leave the table. It says, *I'm done, I'm moving.* You don't borrow stuff. When you first come to prison, people will test you—like, if there are candy bars all over your bed, you don't dive in. You don't take gifts blindly. Your hygiene has to be immaculate. I've seen guys get into physical altercations because one guy wouldn't shower regularly. Prison will teach you good hygiene. Also, you lay off the telephone and the TV when you're new, those are two things that everyone wants to use. They're the things that get guys in trouble the most. Oh, and when you're in the chow line, you don't stand too close to someone. You got some guy up on your back, you might think it's a sexual advance. You gotta respect people's space or you'll be in a world of trouble."

"Wow," I said when Kearse had finished. Most of that ought to be enforced in college dormitories, it struck me. I asked, "And did you ever get into trouble in prison?"

"People didn't really bother me too much," said Kearse, who is bald, tall, and built like a linebacker. "I'd just look at them like, You wanna bring the drama, then I can bring the drama."

## Not an All-Time Low

Many social critics (most of them conservative) will tell you that manners in the Western world have reached an all-time low. Such a viewpoint baffles me. As Swiss sociologist Norbert Elias pointed out in his 1939 masterwork *The Civilizing Process*, prior to the seventeenth and eighteenth centuries people had for millennia burped, spit, and farted in public. Not to mention urinating and defecating on the street, and at the dinner table. It was only then that they began to worry about their appearance—maybe some of the more unsavory portraits in *The Canterbury Tales* had, by this point, cut a little too close to the bone?—and began to clean up their acts.

The fact that few of these critics can agree on what spelled the demise of civility would seem to weaken their argument. The list of culprits is wide ranging—Yale law professor Stephen L. Carter blames the year 1965; *Eats, Shoots & Leaves* author Lynne Truss blames the rise of celebrity as the measure of social status; a recent *New York Times* op-ed blames YouTube; a blogger named Todd Terwilliger writes, "Maybe it all ended when we stopped wearing hats"; a woman who once sat next to me on a plane blamed, in descending order of malignity, rap music, TV dinners, tight pants, and "Brisketty Spears."

One of the more elaborate explanations has come from sociologist Richard Sennett, who teaches at the London School of Economics and New York University. In his 1977 book *The Fall of Public Man*, Sennett posits that our need to be intimate and emotionally expressive with acquaintances and strangers has discredited the value of restraint. "People mostly talk about themselves now. Their calling card is their psyche," Sennett told me when I visited him at his office at NYU. "The notion that you show other people without any restraint your intimate feelings is to say that those feelings don't matter to you."

I asked Sennett—who thinks that the ideal public life was embodied in the coffeehouse culture of 1750s Paris and London—how we might mend our ways. "It's partly a question of how you talk to people. If I say, 'I hate health care. Don't you hate health care?' then you don't have a discussion. That's an agree or disagree, which is no way to learn anything. If you ask someone, 'What do you think?' then it opens up a lot of possibilities."

All these explanations for the demise of manners notwithstanding, I would contend that good manners are, and have been for some years, on the upswing. Sure, cell phones and the anonymity of the Internet have been huge boons to the egoists out there. But if we consider the broader view, as Elias's historical perspective would have us do, we emerge with a different picture: I'd far prefer to eat in a restaurant where everyone is talking on his cellphone than in almost any tavern during the Middle Ages. If the goal is to keep your food down, I mean.

When we look at the history of manners, we see two dominant forms: those that are morals writ in miniature (e.g., waiting for someone to stop talking before responding), and those that are codes of behavior meant to exclude lessers (e.g., speaking in a foreign language that not all in attendance speak). There have been just as many examples of the latter as the former, as Mark Caldwell points out in his book *A Short History of Rudeness*; but I would argue that here in twenty-first-century America— excluding the occasional exotic subculture—we traffic almost exclusively in the small-scale, hold-the-door-for-the-woman-carrying-the-entire-contents-of-her-local-Costco stuff.

This is refreshing. As Caldwell tells it, in the past manners have almost always served as "tokens of solidarity in a distinct human group which—if status is high enough—can decree anything polite by fiat." Caldwell writes of a sixteenth-century aristocratic German tradition whereby Christmas revelers festively pelted one another with dog turds at the dinner table. He also tells us that the Aztecs thought that the careful, class-based assigning of cannibalized body parts (Montezuma, one thigh; the priests, the blood; the commoners, the rib cage) rendered this carnage civil to its participants. "A mannerly custom's real function is to bond the group together," Caldwell writes. "As such, it needs only to be recognizable and distinctive; its moral content is irrelevant."

Sure, modern America still has its occasional Aztec rituals. A letter written by a Youngstown, Ohio, bride to her bridal party in 1976—though it could have been written yesterday—has grown justly infamous, partly because of its deluded approach to hierarchy. "Dear Bridal Party," it starts. "From time to time I will be dropping everyone a line or two to keep each of you informed about how the wedding plans are progressing so that no one thinks I have forgotten them…"

God forbid. To be forgotten by this woman would be to be deprived of a fascinating case study of early-stage dementia.

Bridesmaids: Each bridesmaid will receive her dress via mail from Priscilla of Boston sometime in January. This will give each of you enough time to have the dress "professionally" altered if need be. The dresses are chiffon "Priscilla" dresses and can be worn after the wedding. The right shoulder is

bare and there is no sleeve on the left arm. Each has
its own cape, which goes almost to the floor. The
two matrons of honor will be in silver and the four
bridesmaids in peppermint green. As of this date, I
have not decided whether the two in silver will wear
green gloves and the four in green silver gloves, but
long gloves will be worn. I strongly suggest that
each person shops now for the typical cloth "closed-
toe" shoe. Keep the heel size reasonable—of course,
no platforms of any kind. Anyone having trouble
with their legs should wear support hose.

Ushers: Each usher will be dressed identically to
the groom, best man, and the head groomsman:
black tails. Be sure you have black silk socks and
black dressed shoes polished to a shine.

Though it isn't clear whether or not she intended
her ushers' socks to be buffed to a gleam, her stance on
maquillage proves far more certain:

Dress Requirements: Makeup—It is requested that
you wear a little more than usual because of the
photographs and the movie pictures. Any ladies
with short eyelashes are requested to wear either
false eyelashes or to go to a beauty parlor and have
false eyelashes put in one by one. The matrons of
honor wearing the silver dresses must have a lot of
pink in their makeup. That is straight from Priscilla.

Be sure that each of the other four bridesmaids has green eyeshadow and that everyone wears blusher, powder, eyebrow pencil, foundation, lipstick and mascara—the works!! As for the men, ho, ho, you will have your turn also. If you have a shiny face, be sure to use some of your wife's face powder to take the shine away.

Once suitably done up, the members of the wedding party would at last be able to let their hair down.

Dancing: I will try to find a choreographer to help with the Bridal Dance—but each person can please do his or her part by learning to waltz correctly in three-quarter time. Now, when I say waltz, I do not in any way mean two steps here and two steps there, always standing in one spot. When we waltz it will be to "Tales of the Vienna Woods." Each usher will be twirling his partner while moving in a large circle and maintaining even spacing between each couple. Turn on some old-time movies and you can see how it is supposed to be done. But, PLEASE, PLEASE, practice now! Suggestion: Go take dancing lessons!! That's what we have to do!!

Your dancing lessons will provide you a good opportunity to test-drive your babysitter, whom you'll be needing for this wedding: Kids are *personae non gratae*.

There are many reasons for this request, but the
best is the simple fact that I don't have the money to
invite children who only pick at their food, cry, run
around, etc. One friend of mine, who married about
a year ago, says that when she got her wedding
pictures back, there wasn't one that didn't have a
kid in it and she was disgusted.

Finally, in the grand manner of those who preface
a slam with a compliment so that they can slam even
harder—"I *love* Bob, but…"—our bride kicks off her
closing argument with a gloss at humility.

I know it sounds like I am being a real fusspot, but
I would hate to tell each of you what the cost is per
person just for the reception alone. I'm doing this
for my friends and relatives, for all of us to have a
good time, but since there are only so many hours
in the day, and I already have three jobs, and I am
not a Vanderbilt, some lines must be drawn, and I
hope everyone understands.

I've never wanted a small country-type wedding—
Z. [the fiancé] says this is no wedding but rather a
coronation! Won't each of you come with Z. and
me to fantasyland—a place where dreams come
true and fun abounds for everyone? Where the
bride is Cinderella and the groom is Cinderfella
for an evening. You are going to attend a ball at

"Buckingham Palace" (pretend) and the King and
Queen have invited only "royalty"—YOU! This
will be a time to remember the time when you
were courting the person to whom you are now
married—a time to take a second honeymoon.
We want everyone to be as happy as we are and to
rekindle (add extra "fire" to) their own marriages.
If you have a happy marriage now (which I know
you all do), we expect the Palace to be Really
electrified with all that LOVE.

May your every dream come true!

How do I know about this letter? I read about it on
the Internet. Yes, the information superhighway is, on the
one hand, a seeming no-man's-land of manners, a place
to get craaaaaaaaaaaazzzzzzzzeeeeeeee; but on the other
hand, it's a high-surveillance area where many of your
actions will last in perpetuity. Now that so much of our
lives is Googleable, not to mention Facebookable and
taggable, many of us have developed, for good or ill, an
increased self-awareness. The quotient of accountability
has steepened dramatically in the past twenty years: A
rude prank carried out by a teenager in the current day is
much more likely to be documented than it was thirty, or
even twenty, years ago.

Though in many ways they've made us a blander and
more homogeneous culture, TV and film have done their
bit, too, to undermine the power of arbitrary rituals meant

to exclude lessers. Thank you, every episode of a sitcom in which one of the characters joins a new club or goes to Paris, France. Thank you, Diane Keaton saying "van Goc-chh" in *Manhattan*. Additionally, political correctness, despite its occasional obnoxiousness, has probably helped here, too; the very use of the word *lessers* will get me taken sternly to task by my more righteous readers.

And yet, compelling as the evidence of the twenty-first century's relatively high level of civility may be, this doesn't mean that ours is a golden age. Each day we come face-to-face with acts of egoism and with lapses of decorum. Each day we meet someone whose actions embody the phrase "Move along, bub," or who, when giving us his phone number, tells us, "I'm at *one*-nine-one-seven..."

So we cling to what we can. The saying *Think the retort, but utter the apology* helps some to navigate these rocky shoals. Others take solace in Eleanor Roosevelt's "No one can make you feel inferior except yourself."

But in the heat of the etiquette battle, cool heads don't always prevail. I know mine doesn't. Confronted with lapses of etiquette, I am usually resigned; but sometimes I am irritated.

And, very occasionally, I am pig-biting mad.

# III

*Being an explanation of the author's call to
arms, which same call to arms prompted
a national dragnet of bad manners that
we perpetrate unawares.*

My own conversion point vis-à-vis manners came in 2008, when I conducted an experiment in retaliatory manners. Prior, I was someone who suffered silently at the hands of the impolite and insensitive. But a series of incidents prompted me to start practicing a strange form of activism I might call "reverse etiquette." Namely, I started supplying the apologies that others failed to give me.

It started at the checkout of my local grocery store. The otherwise genial young woman who was ringing up my purchases dropped my apple on the ground, then smiled nervously and picked the apple up and put it in my bag. She said nothing during this, so I offered, in a neutral tone of voice, "Oh, I'm sorry." This did not elicit the remorse I hoped it would—she simply grimace-smiled and said, "That's okay." So I mused, "Sorry about that—I really didn't mean for you to drop that." At which point she stared off into the mid-distance as if receiving instructions from outer space.

A few weeks later, the skinny twenty-something guy manning the cash register at a pizzeria told me, "I can't break a twenty." So I asked, in a tone that was rhetorical and more generous than warranted, "Would you mind terribly if I went next door and got change?" He said, "That's fine." When I returned, no thanks or apology forthcoming from him, I said in a flat, non-sarcastic voice, "So sorry—I hope I didn't keep you waiting?" Confused, he shook his head no. "I forget stuff sometimes," I said—a cue that landed with a splat on the floor.

How had it come to this? I'd feel like a scold or a marm if I told a stranger he had bad manners, so instead I'd opted to wage a campaign of subtle remonstrance. That this subtle remonstrance was, in its initial forays at least, lost on its intended audience did not faze me: Sublimating my irritation was its own reward.

You see, I liked to imagine that by making others wonder what the hell I'm going on about, I might inject them with a toxin called There But for the Grace of God Go I. It's my hope that the person I apologize to when she drops my apple is a person who will have an epiphany the next time someone drops *her* apple. Sometimes we don't see the lesson offered us until it's our turn to be the lesson giver. Whereupon it's like the scene in the thriller when our hero zooms in on a grainy black-and-white photo and realizes that the frowzy grandmother in the back of the photo *is the serial killer before he had a sex change.*

Still, sometimes I am not entirely mollified by improving others' lives with gentle, time-released lessons. Sometimes, the angry little man inside me wants more. Such as, an apology. But I had not yet met Randy Kearse, so the *I'll fuck you up, bitch* prison death-stare had not yet enriched my repertoire.

I started getting more explicit, even aggressive, in my applications of reverse etiquette. One day I apologized to a tall, bearded man who slammed his duffel bag into my not-generally-in-the-way posterior, at Sixth Avenue and 8th Street.

I added, "I'm saying what you should be saying."

His response, in toto: "Oh, right."

These two syllables were hardly contrition. Nevertheless, they gave me enough ground to see that I was on the right track. I realized I just needed to be more explicit with people. Like a judge, I needed to explain the sentence before handing it down. As Margaret Visser reminds us, invoking Dante in *The Gift of Thanks: The Roots and Rituals of Gratitude*, "At the bottomest circle of hell, the ungrateful are punished by being eternally frozen in the postures of deference they failed to perform during their lifetimes: trapped rigid in enveloping ice, they stand erect or upside down, lie prone, or bow face to feet."

My methodology is less severe. A few weeks after the duffel-in-the-rump incident, when a stroller-pushing mother bumped into me at the very same street intersection—apparently the Bermuda Triangle of manners—I expressed remorse, then added, "No one says 'I'm sorry' anymore, so I do it for them."

"Okay."

"My idea is that if I say I'm sorry, then at least the words have been released into the universe."

She stared at me with equal parts irritation and faint horror, as if I had just asked her to attend a three-hour lecture on the history of crackers.

I continued, "The apology gets said, even if it's not by the right person. It makes me feel better. And maybe you'll know what to say next time."

"Wow," she said. (The tickets for the crackers lecture were two hundred dollars, or five hundred at the door.)

And then, finally, came the words I had been longing for months to hear: "I'll think about it."

## The Collective Unconscious

I'd like to tell you that, in the throes of my reverse apologizing, I was oblivious to how bullishly blunt, or even aggressive, I was. But that would be lying.

Yes, in some instances, I was so caught up that it didn't occur to me that icy politeness is not wholly dissimilar to being briskly scrubbed with an iron brush. But in others, I was aware of how abrasive I was being. And while being abrasive wasn't my point, my desire to avoid being so was not enough of a deterrent to rein me in.

As mentioned earlier, one of the more curious aspects of bad manners is that we almost never think that we ourselves have them. *Other* people have bad manners; we just have occasional bad days. *Other* people act in ways that are maliciously thoughtless; we're momentarily preoccupied, so sorry about that, I wasn't thinking, I only got three hours of sleep last night, I've had a *crazy* week, didn't mean to bite your head off.

Oscar Wilde offers us, in his deft way, a neat excuse: "A gentleman is one who never hurts another's feelings unintentionally." As I was being *deliberately* horrendous to these strangers and tradespersons, I could reassure myself that I was not being ungentlemanly.

Over the years, my own examples of I-wasn't-thinkings have been legion. I might cite the wedding present I made for two friends shortly after I graduated from college. They were living illegally in a commercial space—his photography studio—and, each morning after breakfast, they had to hide all evidence of their living in, and having slept in, the studio. I had little money those days, so when it came time to get these friends a wedding present, I knew I'd have to get creative. For reasons that now escape me, I thought it would be the height of hilarity to write a little storybook with pictures—I enjoy cutting out photos from magazines and used books, and then pasting them into a blank book and then captioning them so that they tell a story—that likened my two friends' hideaway life to that of Anne Frank. My two Jewish friends, in point of fact. My job at the time was in a tiny office, where I worked with the wife of this couple; you can imagine the staggering awkwardness that pervaded those four hundred square feet on the Monday morning that, stern-faced, she told me she had opened my present and found it "a little strange." Even my *watch* stopped ticking.

Or consider the time that my then-boyfriend asked me to Maine for a weekend at the house of his charming, slightly-brighter-and-shinier-than-me friend. It probably would have been initially disappointing, but ultimately fine with him, had I politely declined, crying deadlines and a heavy work schedule. But instead I squeezed out a "Sure," thus inciting the boyfriend to buy plane tickets, reserve a car, and make restaurant reservations for dinner at an inn one night. The Friday morning of our takeoff, my boyfriend appeared at my doorstep, luggage in hand, smile on face. At which point—prompted by jealousy of the friend, or by entropy, I'm not sure—I waffled. "I'm not sure I can come," I said. Accusations, tears, strangled yelling: Such were the hallmarks of his response. Which, in turn, were followed by my own versions of same. (Ultimately, his subsequent outburst and tears made me waffle on the waffle; we went, and had a lovely time. But the fun had is actually beside the point. I had acted badly, prompting him to act even worse, and the whole contre-temps could have been avoided by a moment's thought. Thought and resolve.)

Yes, these two examples, like my reverse apologizing, are fairly glaring. Yet surely there have been hundreds—a person who's known me twenty years breaks in enthusi-astically to say "thousands"—of times I violated Wilde's law: I unknowingly hurt peoples' feelings, or induced awkwardness, or acted high-handedly, or pushed my way to the front of the line.

Sometimes these misdeeds occur when you're having the most fun.

## Touch the Waiter

I play the game called Touch the Waiter. You see who at your table can touch the waiter the greatest number of times without the waiter's figuring out you're doing so.

Often the game is prompted by the attentions of a waiter who is overly present—a waiter whose description of the porcini risotto involves the kind of nostril quiver-ing one encounters in coffee commercials.

But sometimes you touch because to touch is to love: You make this particular form of brief, tactile contact with a stranger in the same way that you might laugh at her joke, or tell him that his is the best impersonation of a parrot eating peanut butter you've ever seen.

I don't tell you about this game because I'm hoping to make you feel wildly uncomfortable should you and I ever break bread. Rather, I hope to point out how someone's sense of fun—in this case, my own—can sometimes engender its own obliviousness.

Touch the Waiter, like all good games, operates with a code of honor: The touch is never wanton, nor directed at the sullen or the insecure. It never results from your finding the waiter attractive, or from your needing a place to rest your weary hands. The touched waiter should generally be the recipient of a better-than-adequate tip—not because you touched her, but because you liked her, as a person, well enough to touch in the first place.

The venue for one of my early games was Lunenburg, Nova Scotia, at a charming if slightly precious seafood house. So impassioned and doting were Edward's greeting and recitation of the dinner specials that a bodily response from us four diners seemed warranted, nay called for. When Edward helped one of my fellow diners to unfold her napkin, we knew we wanted not merely to touch Edward, but also to buff and possibly floss Edward. And so one of my tablemates and I launched into an escalating series of subtle elbow caresses and arm taps, all delivered in the context of deeply felt appreciation. (I lost, 3–4. And that was when I realized that points for style had to count in the final tallies.)

I've played in both crowded dive bar and becalmed, four-star foodie temple; in small groups and in large. At La

Grenouille, the last of New York's great, old-guard, haute French restaurants, I touched my waiter—sixtyish, Latin, brimming with a desire to please—twice, but only after my dining companion and I had stood up to leave. A touch administered on departure has a much lower degree of difficulty than an early-onset-of-meal or even a mid-meal one; on scorecards worldwide, this is a half-lutz. But it should be pointed out that the reduced points reflect the amount of time a player has had to establish rapport, and not the fact that he is on his feet: The player who stands during the meal and manages to engineer away-from-table physical contact with the server is a player who is now familiar with the ratcheting thrum of Verdi's Triumphal March.

Not everyone is eager to board the touch train, of course. When I dine with my boyfriend, for instance, I am forced to play solitaire. It's a smaller game, a quieter game; a game that usually goes unannounced until it's under way. Recently Greg and I had dinner at an Italian place in Soho called Giorgione. Just seconds after the jovial, fifty-something waiter had handed us our menus and gone to get water, this player was able to report to Greg that I was "on the board."

Greg rolled his eyes slightly heavenward. Upon the arrival of the entrées, I got in a tiny elbow nuzzle while exclaiming over my angel-hair. By the time my new friend had gone off in search of pepper, I updated Greg, "I'm two for two." Greg, with a look of indulgence, mock-chanted, "USA! USA!"

After the waiter had supplied us with dessert, I held up three fingers for Greg's inspection. Staring at them, and then at our server's back as it disappeared into the kitchen, Greg asked, "How do you think the waiter feels if he figures out you're doing this?"

I considered that question briefly, but waited a good while to answer, so as to connote deep reflection.

"I think you've gotta be flattered," I offered, "especially if you're from a Latin country."

"As all Alfords are."

"No, I mean if *the waiter* is."

"I knew what you meant."

But how *did* the waiter feel? That had come up before. In my mind I checked a box marked "Depends on Situation."

In another case, I've tried to propagate my odd restaurant behavior in someone else—to give the gift of touch, as it were. I'd pegged my assistant Ryan—a recent college graduate who does a lot of comedy improv—as a potential Toucher; but when I broached the topic with him, Ryan became giggly and unsettled, as if in the presence of a dancing bear.

One afternoon, seated at Dojo, a low-key, folksy restaurant in the vicinity of New York University, I told Ryan that I had just touched our waitress. Ryan's expression was one of curiosity, slight longing: a venture capitalist who's been told there's something very exciting happening just beneath the crust of the earth.

But when our server brought our meals, he lapsed back into stasis.

"I missed my shot," he said once she'd gone. I counseled, "Don't force it. Let it come to *you*."

But after two more appearances by the waitress, Ryan, still uninitiated, confessed, "I feel bad."

"Don't," I said. "However, you may want to practice with the home game." Ryan, who lives with his parents, said to the air, "Uh, Mom..."

A few weeks later, we found ourselves in more propitious circumstances, at Noho Star, a fairly bustling bistro-type restaurant near my office. I asked our server—vivacious, in her late twenties, lots of curly hair—whether she'd ever heard of Touch the Waiter. She hadn't, so I explained, "Various people sitting together in a restaurant try to touch the waiter without the waiter's becoming aware of it."

"Okay."

"Just a tap on the elbow or a brief shoulder clap."

"Unh-huh."

"I was wondering...Well, I've been trying to get Ryan here into the spirit of it but he hasn't plunged yet." I deftly veered away from the phrase *been blooded*. "He still has his training wheels on. Would it be all right if he, uh, touched you, just so he can get in the game?"

The instant the words came out of my mouth, I felt a flush come over my cheeks, as when you stand up from your seat and realize you've just drunk four glasses of wine. I remembered someone at the first magazine where I'd worked saying, "All editorial assistants must undergo a ritual deflowering."

The waitress smiled and said, "Sure."

Ryan patted her forearm.

We all breathed a sigh of relief.

The waitress headed back to the kitchen.

But: Ten minutes later, a second waitress—thin, attractive, in her thirties—approached our table to clear our dishes and asked suspiciously, "Are you the Touch Me guys?"

*Oh my God. They've put out an APB on us.*

"Uh, yeah," I said, hoping to sound more offhand than sheepish. "Are you...were you looking for a game?"

"I'm a little freaked out by it, actually." Grabbing the plates while keeping a good yard back from the table, she rushed off.

We crept out of the restaurant like two new neighbors who'd just spotted each other on a Megan's Law site.


## The Listening List

Fortunately, I am not alone. Though most people are able to keep their hands to themselves when dining out, many of us commit unconscious lapses of etiquette every day.

Some of these bad manners are universally agreed upon. Let us all now, as a group, raise our middle finger to

drivers who don't use their directional signal when passing; to people who attend their cell phones with attention
more befitting an adorable and possibly sickly dachs-
hund. Because these infamies are so iconic in nature, I'm
not going to harp on them too extensively; it is sufficient
to point out their existence. These fish—and the barrel
that contains them—need not be dignified with further
gunfire.

Still, we might ask: What are some of the commonly
overlooked unpleasantries that we commit each day,
without even knowing it? Let's consider these *not* in an
effort to make us all more neurotic, but to show how on
occasion, we can all be oblivious to the things everyone
else wishes we would stop doing.

Over the course of six months or so, I asked a large
number of friends and colleagues (plus several random
acquaintances) to tell me what bad manners (outside of
the aforementioned directives regarding cell phones and
vehicular directionals) are most egregiously committed
unawares.

Here are the results of my listening tour.

1. **The "No Problem" Problem.** This was perhaps
the most surprising example to me—both because it was
the most widely cited, and because it's something I myself
have been known to say. To wit: Many of us use "No
problem" as a substitute for "You're welcome," "My pleasure," or the Palin-esque, "You betcha!" I didn't quite

understand why anyone would so vehemently object to the use of this phrase, until I e-mailed an acquaintance one day to say, "Hey, great running into you last night. So sorry I couldn't make it to your party." To which she replied, in toto, "No problem." My brain sputtered. *No problem?* How could my non-presence at her gathering be even remotely construed as a "problem"? Have I been dandruffing on the guacamole again?

The use of "No problem" as a replacement for "You're welcome" or "Don't give it a thought!" is probably valid only in situations where there may actually *be* a problem—e.g., your interlocutor has, by knocking on your door and asking to use your phone, roused you in the middle of a particularly vivid dream about Winston Churchill asking you what to do about the Germans. Or he has requested—in a sudden emergency—the loan of your grandfather's violin for a concert to be held outdoors in the rain.

Be warned, however, if it is your *job* to provide service to the person who is thanking you—e.g., if you have just scooped his ice cream and are now drowning it in choco-accessories ("No problem, sir!"). Or if here under the fluorescent lights you have made a printout of his annuities portfolio. Or if you have *not* been interrupted, interrogated, violated, or pressed in any way, and are simply saying "No problem" to be self-effacingly heroic. You might be trafficking in implied martyrdom.

2. **PGRs.** Each time I pass them weekly in the hall, three people in my "daily circuit" (i.e., my apartment building or my office building) fail to make even the most Perfunctory Gestural Recognition of my presence. A smile, a tilt of the head, a pucker of the lips, a wave of the fingers—even a full-bore "Hello." Any of these can be calling cards.

3. **Match Your Meet.** In the communication hierarchy surrounding phone call/e-mail/text/social networking site, you generally want to match the level of the incoming vehicle or move up the hierarchy—but not down. Answering a phone call with an e-mail can look like you're trying to avoid something or someone; answering an e-mail with a Facebook message looks like you've been lobotomized by a doctor whose office is located in Farmville.

4. **All Is Less.** Actor and writer Colleen Werthmann wondered why anyone "Replies All on a group informational e-mail, only to make a non-essential comment like 'Great, thanks.'" Werthmann said, "That is like a pixilated version of a Styrofoam peanut."

5. **Who's That Girl?** Esther Pica, a friend of mine from high school, recently took her goddaughter to the zoo and fell into conversation with one of the moms

milling about. When Esther told the woman that she was hoping to teach young Eva some Spanish, the mother pronounced Esther "*perfect*," and asked how much Esther "got per week," and if she did light housekeeping. Esther— who, unlike her goddaughter, is black—sputtered, "I don't do this for money!" whereupon the mother said, "Obviously, you do this because you love children!" Esther explained to the woman that she was Eva's godmother. Whereupon the woman again offered to hire Esther. Moral: Don't assume that a woman of color who is playing with a white baby is being paid to do so.

6. **What Do You Don't.** On being introduced to a new person and learning her profession, try not to instantly invoke the name of the leading or most famous practitioner in that field, even if the field is obscure and to do so is to show your dazzling hipness or interrelatedness. Just because your sister-in-law is the number one Realtor in the tristate area, or just because you've recently watched an appearance by a celebrity dog groomer on the *Today* show doesn't mean that either of these facts needs to be your opening salvo when meeting someone who works in real estate or dog beautification. The person you were introduced to might be number 2 in that field, or even number 37 or number 5,348, and feel that your name-dropping diminishes her. This risks setting off a series of associations that amble down the garden path to the compost heap of "I am a big fat loser." Instead,

perhaps you could employ some other arrow from your quiver. Say, curiosity.

**7. Drugstore Restraint.** If you see someone you know in a pharmacy or drugstore, it's typically best to steer clear of him. He may be buying condoms or hemorrhoidal salves, or any of a host of unguents meant to bring relief or pleasure to the body's carapaces and byways. Is this something you want to shine a bright light on?

**8. Department Store Restraint.** If you see someone wearing a navy blazer staring listlessly at the floor in a department store, do not assume she is a salesperson. Ask, "Have you seen a salesperson?"

**9. The Drop-Off.** If you're driving a friend to his car late at night, train your headlights on his car until he has gotten into his car, started it, and commenced driving. Post-completion "sparkle fingers" optional.

**10. The Show Business.** It's fascinating to me how many administrators, business folk, writers, and artists will, when standing in front of a group of people who have assembled expressly to hear them speak, act in a way that suggests that the situation is a surprise to them.

Could they, prior to addressing the group, put a Post-it in their book so that they might easily access the section they'll be reading from? Or perhaps their pie-chart graph could be, as is said in the theater, "pre-set"? I grant you, performing and public speaking are terrifying. But a few preparatory steps might soothe the nerves of these easily sidetracked, flustered *a-hem*ers.

Admittedly, an air of high distractedness can occasionally be charming—if you're Joaquin Phoenix receiving the blah-blah-d'Or at Cannes; or if you're so moved by the motional tenor of the proceedings that it's difficult for you to speak. But in almost all other situations, we'll admire preparedness and succinctness. Brevity kills.

11. **Pregnant or Well-Fed?** No individual should congratulate a woman on her pregnancy until that woman has announced that she is indeed pregnant: Enough of us have been scarred by this faux pas, on both sides of the transaction, that we've been able to get the word out on this. (As a corollary, pregnant women, unless they expressly ask you to do so, do not usually wish to have their bellies touched—especially if you are a complete stranger to them. They're not melon.)

It's less widely known, though, that pregnant women bear the burden of publicizing their pregnant-ness: I have been forced to make myself ridiculous by "ignoring" female acquaintances' eight-month or nine-month swollen bellies, not to mention their discussions of thawed-but-untoasted waffles or entire wheels of Brie that they have consumed at midnight in front of their kitchen sink in roomy lingerie, since I'd not been told these women were pregnant. Until I receive the press release, I can only act as if these ladies are livin' large.

12. **Theater Bitching.** Our behavior is often at its worst when we are chastising others' behavior. (Amy Vanderbilt writes in the first edition of her etiquette guide, "Some of the rudest and most objectionable people I have ever known have been technically the most 'correct.'") The classic example is the theater patron whose shushing is louder than the talking or candy unwrapping that unleashed his inner librarian. If an arched eyebrow and a contorted expression of rage do not convey the importance of the situation, then those prone to complaint might bring to the theater a small flashlight with which to briefly illuminate talkers. (See also my reverse-apology campaign.)

13. **Waiting to Go.** Love affairs and acts of passion find us at our most impulsive. When we are compelled to pull away from, or break it off with, another person, we should be careful about timing. If a gentleman breaks off an affair directly after his lover has dyed her hair, she will have the distinct impression that he does not like her as a blonde; if a woman who's in the throes of an assignation sobs "I can't do this anymore!" just as her paramour is removing his underwear, the paramour may be led to believe that his lover does not approve of his man-parts.

14. **All Is Forgiven.** When asking someone for a big-gish favor, it's thoughtful to go through the motions of letting that person off the hook. "I totally understand if this request is awkward or impossible" has a nice ring to it (and, counterintuitively, it may make some people—some people who might not have, otherwise—grant the favor because they don't want to be backed into a corner by the favor-asker and his proverbial staple gun).

15. **"Where Are You Staying?"** If a friend's upcom-ing travels arise in conversation, you might try to avoid asking the question "Where are you staying?" It may set off alarms for those who squirm under the harsh light of status assessment. Indeed, this question seems to call for the answer "The Ritz. I know of no other location." You're better off with "What neighborhood are you staying in?" (Many neighborhoods offer a variety of accommodations at varying prices.) Or perhaps there's something even more general, like "What will you eat?" Or "Do you have enough condoms?"

16. **Faint Praise.** Deanna Larson, who works for the public library in Nashville, said, "Don't walk into some-one's home, apartment, or RV and say 'Well! This has potential!' Because if 'this' is as far as the decorating train goes, it just makes everybody feel bad."

Indeed, damning with faint praise is a time-honored source of discomfort. Note its presence in the statements

"What a dress! It looks so expensive!," "I saw your drawings in that exhibition. They gave you so much space!," "We're just back from China. Very flat, China," and "Sure—I know Eric. Eric is *so human*."

17. **Together Again.** Gatherings present a raft of potential problems. If you are inviting friends or colleagues over largely because you feel obliged to do so or because it is payback, the resultant gathering is likely to be a leaden affair. Why not invite these folks instead to a concert in the park, or a ball game? Or you could buy opera tickets. Or tell them to meet you at an ATM near your house, and when they arrive, spray them with strawberry soda.

In an ideal world, people would be discreet enough not to mention the gatherings they've been invited to or attended in the presence of people who were not invited or did not attend. But, alas, people love to blab about where they've gone and whom they've seen. Therefore, hosts must be judicious when inviting people to gatherings and events—particularly if the party is going to be a large one. If we know that Andrew is in daily communication with Beverly, or that Jose and Erica have become best pals, then we should consider the consequences of inviting only one member of either dyad. If logistics preclude inviting everyone, it's not rude to tell Andrew in so many words that you are inviting him but *not* Beverly, so could he keep his trap shut, please? Conversely, if you *are* inviting both Andrew and Beverly, it might be lovely to send the e-mail jointly, or tell them they're both invited, so awkwardness does not ensue.

If you're having people over for dinner, ask them beforehand what food they can't or don't eat. Or, serve buffet-style. Or serve family-style, with options. In a world in which people mix their own salads and design their own clothing online and buy only the songs they like from a CD, many experience a feeling of sovereignty when handed the reins of their dinner plate. Anyhow, it's less awkward than seeing your boss's wife pick out all the black olives from the plate of chicken tagine you served her, in one of the six beautifully blue-glazed Moroccan bowls you threw out half your socks to bring back.

Francine Maroukian, the food writer and former caterer, says that when you have people to your home, "Answer your own door. Something as simple as that can make people who are unfamiliar feel immediately welcome. And you'll know right away what the state of the guest is and you can decide if they need a little support and who to introduce them to." It's very common in my world to go to the home of someone who has invited twenty or thirty of his friends over, and never once be introduced to another guest by the host. Occasionally, this negligence results from an overworked host. But in most cases the passivity stems from good intentions. Some hosts overestimate the camaraderie of a crowd—"We all live in the same town, and no one in the room is more than two or three degrees of separation away from anyone else in the room, so who needs introductions?" Other hosts don't want to look like they're trying too hard. Still, not introducing your guests to one another is a disservice.

18. **Getting the Nod.** If the invitation is RSVP, then we need to RSVP even if we are not going. This is not commonly practiced. In instances in which events must be kept to a maximum capacity, not RSVPing may actually mean keeping another person from being invited (since people are probably being invited in waves).

"Most people's excuse for not RSVPing is 'Well, I'm a spontaneous person,'" Judith Martin told me, rolling her eyes heavenward. "Well, good luck with that! If I say 'Let's go get a cup of coffee,' are you just going to look at me?"

Sometimes you're invited to events that your partner is not invited to—even by people who know you both. Unless you know the host well, it's usually considered rude to ask to bring someone. The best way to deal with this situation might be to write that you cannot come because you and your partner already have plans for the evening. If the host is adept and really wants you, then she'll invite your partner along, too.

When RSVPing to dinner, Maroukian says, "Don't make your dietary restrictions the hostess's problem. If you have an allergy or religious restriction, that's one thing. But if you're just not in the mood for chervil, then that's not your host's responsibility. Telling your host that you're on a low-fat, carb-free, lactose-intolerant, I-eat-only-green-food-on-Thursday, Billy Bob Thornton diet—that's inappropriate." Caterer Jane McQueen-Mason recalls a guest at a small gathering at someone's house requesting a Coke Zero. "On what *planet* do people keep Coke Zero in their house?" To make such a request can cause a host to lose face.

At gatherings, we should make an effort to talk to anyone who is standing alone, even if their hauteur and/or hairdo is titanic. If the gathering was not wholly impromptu and/or not hosted by someone you see daily, and/or involved something more on the host's part than giving you each a glass of water, we should, sometime within the next few days, write a thank-you note or e-mail.

19. **Blot on the Landscape.** If the person with whom you're conversing is sporting a visible booger, make an excuse to disappear momentarily from his view. Return with two sheets of Kleenex and, looking off into the mid-distance, somewhat sheepishly say, "Apparently you and I both need to blow our noses." Then proceed to do so. The theory behind this has broad application: By making any embarrassment seem mutual, you reduce its sting.

20. **You're Losing Interest.** My nephew Adam Eltorai suggested, "If you receive a check, deposit it within a couple of weeks." Unaccountability bedevils accountancy.

21. **Kids Today.** Brad Gendell, a hedge fund manager in New York City, and his wife, Yfat Reiss Gendell, a literary agent, are the new parents of twins. They said, "We loathe people who say things like 'Sleep now! You won't sleep after the babies come!,' or who say, with a foreboding tone, 'Your life will never be the same.' Why would you say that? Why not be encouraging?"

22. **Try This.** It's not uncommon for friends of cancer patients to send suggested remedies or regimes for their ill friends to pursue. Tucker Melancon, a US district court judge who has had nine rounds of chemo and thirty-three rounds of radiation for his breast cancer, said, "You get inundated. 'I read about this treatment, I saw this one on TV.' You might have a good idea for your friend, but I think it's a mistake to come in like that." Indeed, this kind of good neighbor can easily become a Gladys Kravitz. Mary Cappello, a professor of English at University of Rhode Island who was diagnosed with breast cancer in 2007, said that receiving a regime for a macrobiotic diet from an acquaintance felt accusatory to her: "As if to say *Ultimately, it was your fault. You weren't eating right. That's why this happened.*"

23. **Elder Pestering.** Dr. Ruth, who at eighty-two still writes books and lectures at Princeton and Yale, said that older folks don't want to be repeatedly asked "Are

you okay?" and "Are you happy?" At a certain point, the question sounds like a death rattle. Similarly, people with terminal illnesses don't want to hear "You look great!" more than seven times an hour. The statement's opposite—"You look cancerous!"—is no better. (A colleague, on telling her mother-in-law that she had breast cancer, was met with the wail "Oh, your beautiful children!")

But perhaps you could shift the spotlight altogether. Most people in hospitals don't want klieg lights, they want the current issue of *People*.

## IV

*A ritual goes awry, prompting the author to elucidate some of the rudeness we enact specific to particular jobs.*

Approximately 280 mornings each year, during 2008 and 2009, I bought one copy of *The New York Times* and one copy of the *New York Post* at a certain newsstand located near my office in New York City. Reading the paper is my morning ritual: Some people like to lie in bed listening to the clock radio, I like to make my fingers look like I've been eating charcoal.

The person who manned the newsstand's counter most mornings was a grim, middle-aged gentleman I'll call Lou. Lou's warmth was less than incandescent; on the rare occasion that he acknowledged you personally, he didn't so much return your greeting as toss it back like a live grenade.

But two of Lou's other traits loomed larger in my

mind: He was possibly the most exhausted-looking person I've ever beheld, and he was always wearing a tracksuit. Had Lou jogged to work from a neighboring state? Had Lou stayed up all night, fine-tuning his "gruff"? Was Lou teaching an aerobics class at dawn that met in front of the cigarette display? I did wonder.

It was usually about nine AM when I stumbled into Lou's domain, where I'd absentmindedly plop my two papers down on the counter, one on top of the other, the larger *New York Times* ($2.00) generally overlying the smaller *New York Post* (50 cents); I'd fumble in my trousers for $2.50. After I'd done this some two months, I noticed: While I was groping myself for change, Lou was gently lifting my papers from the counter in order to see whether there was a third paper or other entity in the pile.

Offended, I said nothing.

But when I returned the next day, I started something new: I would get Lou's attention by holding each paper up in the air and shaking it slightly to demonstrate its freestanding-ness and un-encumbrance—a kind of nonerotic shimmy. Lou would merely blink or nod in recognition. Once the two papers were down on the counter, however, Lou stared at the neat stack ominously, as if surveilling one of those insects that can reproduce without congress.

After I'd enacted my airborne presentation enough times to constitute a pattern of behavior, I noticed Lou staring at my papers one morning. So I genially asked him, "You think I'm trying to hide a magazine or third paper under there, don't you?"

"No, no," he said, shaking his head unconvincingly.

A few weeks later, it happened again: Lou looked down at my presentation as if awaiting the arrival of dancing mites or two-inch-high Scottish bagpipers. He reached out with his right hand to start dislodging, but I beat him to the punch by setting my hand firmly on the *Times*.

"You and I both know what's under there," I said.

Lou, unblinkingly: "Yes."

"Is it French *Vogue*?"

"No…"

"Is it the new issue of *Cat Fancy*?"

"Uh?" The reference was at first obscure to him, but then it clicked: "No."

"So why are we having this conversation?"

"Sorry, guy. Sometimes you buy the gum."

It was true—occasionally I bought the gum. But didn't I always put the gum on top of the papers?

Ten months later, having switched allegiances to another newsstand, I fell into conversation with this new newsstand's proprietor, whom I'll call Brian. I told Brian—a chatty, friendly Indian man in his late thirties— the Lou story.

Brian smiled awkwardly and said, "But you *do* sometime bury magazines between the newspapers."

"I do?"

"Yes. *Entertainment Weekly. Us. Time.*"

He was absolutely right. I never think of these purchases because they are irregular and impulsive.

I thought back on my months of buying from Lou and realized that I'd been sleep-buying these magazines then, too.

A few days later, I swung by Lou's newsstand to acknowledge my gaffe, but I was told Lou had moved out of the city. In my mind I pictured a blur of gray—Lou's tracksuit—and then that tiny cloud of dust you see when Wile E. Coyote falls off a butte and into the Grand Canyon.

Chastened, a few weeks later I told a friend about the two newsstands. "I feel like I'm wearing orthopedic shoes," I said. She shot me a look of incomprehension, so I explained, "I stand corrected."

## Rude Questions

Some manners dilemmas, as my experience with Lou suggests, are job-specific: They result from the unique scenarios that arise around a particular job, or from the general public's ignorance of the specific duties and challenges of that line of work.

In my own life, three or four times a year, I encounter someone who asks me, "Did I just read something of yours?"—a statement that causes me to look down at the floor as if in search of my imaginary friend, Mr. Buttons. They'll continue, "I feel like I just read something of yours, and I can't remember what it was." (Once, apropos of a radio piece I'd recorded about struggling painters and sculptors, an acquaintance told me, "I think I heard you on the radio the other day? Talking about tightrope walkers maybe?")

These kinds of comments used to hurt my feelings. But gradually, I devised a series of responses meant to deflate the situation. For a long while I would jest, "Wow, it sounds like my article really colonized your imagination." Once, having practiced in advance, I offered, "That statement has all the earmarks of a compliment, but without any of the discomfiting specificity of one." (I can be, as I may have mentioned, an ass.)

In only one case have I been moved to tackle the insensitivity head-on. I told a journalism student—because I thought that it was a valuable skill for him to have in his arsenal—that he shouldn't proffer a vague compliment like "I think I read something of yours" to someone in his field: "If you can't remember, then say nothing. Or just say, 'I like your work.'"

At this point, the "did I just read your piece" comment doesn't faze me so much—though I am continually amazed by just who utters such a comment: people who are in the same boat as me (other creative types), and people who are in the "people" trade (publicists, agents, strippers). As the stand-up comics say, *How's that workin' for ya?*

But I'm not alone, of course. Teachers and professors are regularly asked by their students, upon return from an absence, "Did I miss anything?" This would seem to suggest that, on some days, the class consists of nothing more than staring silently at the classroom's doorknob for three hours. Additionally, those who teach—particularly at the college level—are also regularly asked about, if not taken to task for, having summers off. But as Sheila Fisher, who teaches English at Trinity College in Hartford, Connecticut, puts it, "Professors don't get summers off—that's the time they get to do the research that's one of the important reasons they became professors in the first place and is the reason they will, come September, have something to 'profess.'"

Most cabdrivers who are born in foreign countries dislike being asked where they're from. "I'm American," Daniel Kebede, a cabbie who drove me in Washington, DC, told me. "I'm *from* Ethiopia, but I'm American." (When forced to provide an answer to this question, Kebede will sometimes mumble, "I'm from Planet Earth.") Like the comments "Your English is excellent" and "You're so articulate," the question "Where are you from?" can sound more anthropological than friendly.

Even priests get caught in the cross-hairs. The Reverend Carmen Mele, a Catholic priest in Fort Worth, Texas, said he had a pious aunt who would request a mass for a dead friend, and then ask her nephew how much the mass would cost. "I tried to explain that we cannot put a price on mass intentions, and would then go into the issue of stipends, which are set by individual dioceses to avoid simony, the selling of things sacred."

Yet people continue to ply Father Mele with the question "How much will the mass cost?" Mele said, "The correct answer to this query is 'The passion and death of Jesus of Nazareth, the God-human.'"

Eager to find out what other kinds of rude questions—besides the obvious "How much money do you make?"—are being leveled at innocent bystanders, I hit the pavement and Internet, accompanied by my non-waiter-touching colleague, Ryan Haney.

Our findings suggest to me that these forms of ignorance tend to fall into one of five categories. I don't include in these five categories a certain kind of remark—asking of a psychiatrist, "But how do you *really* feel?" or of an undertaker, "How's business?"—because the people making such remarks should probably be chastised more for witlessness than a lack of manners. (Joseph O'Sullivan, a detective sergeant in Niles, Illinois, when asked what rude questions he's received, responded, "Donuts: how much I like them, why we're always eating them, do we get them for free.")

The first circle of rudeness encompasses all comments that question or call into doubt the very existence of the job at hand. Like, asking a storeowner why she's in business given that everything she sells is available and cheaper online; or asking a lifeguard if his bathing suit has ever touched water. These comments might be sharp and direct—James Latzel, a lighting designer in New Britain, Connecticut, has been asked, "People pay you to do that?" Alternatively such comments might take the form of a barbed compliment. Many waiters, including New York City's Darren Cardosa, have been subject to the age-old query "But what do you *really* do?"

The people who ask "But what do you really do?" tend to feel they're on safe ground if their interlocutor is in her twenties. They really aren't, though. What if the person is actually a career waiter, or someone who has not yet emerged from the career chrysalis?

Sylvie Kim, a graduate student at San Francisco State, recalled going to a friend's birthday party at a posh Financial District watering hole. A white gentleman who worked in the defense industry, on being told that Kim was getting her master's in Asian American studies, asked, "But why would you need to study that?" Quashing her impulse to ask the gentleman, *Why would you need to wear those fugly pants?* Kim instead launched into an impassioned response: "There is no Asian monolith that has come to this country to do your math and deliver your Chinese food! Everything from policy to community resources to how we appear on TV sitcoms is significant! The Model Minority myth has screwed us, but as scholars and engaged citizens we can start to dismantle these deeply embedded images!" Kim got halfway through her tirade before realizing that the gentleman really didn't care about what she was saying—"My defense of Asian American studies was just killing his party buzz." Later that evening, Kim realized what she wished she'd said: The reason I have to stand here and explain the significance of Asian American studies is the reason there needs to be Asian American studies. And those pants look stupid.

Sometimes questions in this category betray a certain amount of knowledge on the interrogator's behalf. Kent Wien, who lives in Boston and has nearly twenty years of experience as a domestic and international pilot for a major airline, is sometimes asked, "So aren't airliners pretty much automated? I mean, you don't really have to do much, do you?"

As Wien explained, "While it's true that there's far more automation in our airplanes compared with those flown during my grandpa's or even my father's career, often that automation comes with a lot of new training requirements and procedures." Also: "No airplane is capable of taking off with the use of an autopilot."

Like Wien, fashion blogger Asma Q. Parvez, whose site is called *Haute Muslimah*, is forced to defend her work from time to time. When people ask the Austin, Texas, resident why she blogs, she tells them, "Well, I'm a mother and wife, and blogging is something I do for myself."

Parvez added that the next question in such an encounter is usually "So what's your real job?"

"That's pretty much it."

"What do you—a Muslim—know about fashion?"

"I was born and raised here in the United States. My mom's actually American, and I just picked up on it."

"What's Islamic fashion?"

"Muslim women want to wear trendy, fashionable clothing," she'll explain—trendy, fashionable clothing that falls within Muslim dictates. "I follow what's on trend through fashion shows, magazines, and what I'm noticing is popular. I then do my best to translate that in a way that I feel a Muslim woman would feel comfortable wearing."

"What the heck is that thing on your head?"

"It's called a hijab, and I wear it to cover in front of men that I am not related to."

"Is your dad/husband forcing you to wear it?"

"Hah. No, I don't think anyone can force me to do anything I don't want to. I cover of my own free will."

The second type of rudeness leveled at people in the workforce typically assaults the credentials or expertise of the person in question. Herein we might find someone asking a hairdresser how recently he sharpened his scissors, or asking a babysitter if she has ever read Piaget. This type of question is of especial piquancy when the profession in question is centered on the saving of lives. For instance, Angela Haney, a registered nurse in Stamford, Connecticut, is sometimes asked "How long have you been a nurse?," and Robert Rodems, a firefighter and EMT-E in Mechanicsville, Virginia, often gets "What took you so long to get here?" (The irony is not lost on Rodems that "Typically, when it's not their emergency, citizens often criticize how fast we drive.")

No less off-base are queries that betray an inability to tell whether someone is working or not. "Clients will occasionally ask 'Are you billing me for this call?'" says Jaime Wolf, a lawyer in New York City. "I have to explain to them that, yes, I make my livelihood billing people for the time I spend listening to their problems and helping solve them. But my first impulse is always to say 'You're damn right I am!'"

Category III questions betray their formulators' unrealistic expectations about a line of work, and may range from the slightly misguided (Marcela Valdes, a book critic from Annapolis, Maryland: "Who's the most famous person you've ever slept with?") to the outright loopy (Sean Zimmer, who has worked as a farmhand in Charlottesville, Virginia: "Do you milk the boy cows, too?").

Perhaps unsurprisingly, these odd expectations usually come from the media, or are *about* jobs in the media. Katie Budge of San Francisco, on telling people that she's an actress, has been asked, "Really? So why haven't I heard of you?"; Ef Rodriguez, a social media strategist in Boulder, Colorado, said, "'So, you probably don't have a life, right?' That's the question I've received most often from students, acquaintances, and people in lateral professions. I'm paid to develop social media strategy.

As a consequence, I spend an enormous amount of time online—building relationships, unearthing nascent trends and memes, and staying sure-footed in a digital environment that can shift overnight. The charge that my profession robs me of a 'life' is pretty obnoxious and far from the truth."

Given their relative glamorousness, the jobs in this category may generate a whole slew of questions about the work, as opposed to a single surgical strike about donut consumption. This fusillade of questioning may obscure an important point. Allie Kokesh worked until recently as an NBC page in Los Angeles, a job brought to national prominence by Jack McBrayer's portrayal of goofy Kenneth the page on *30 Rock*. Kokesh didn't mind a lot of the queries that her livelihood begets: "I was typically asked, 'Do you wear the blue blazer?' It's now a gray Brooks Brothers suit. 'Do you get paid?' Yes, but only ten dollars an hour. 'Are you just like Kenneth?' Definitely. But when my career status was followed by 'Oh, yeah, I wanna do that, who do I send my résumé to?,' I was offended. I was in the application process for nearly a year. I'd been told they can't even look at a lot of the résumés that flood the program's inbox. The ease with which someone says 'Yeah, I'd like to try the chocolate flavor,' should not be the same feeling one has for applying for my job."

A fourth category of question sees someone lodging odd or unnecessary demands on his listener. With this kind of query, presumptuousness cross-breeds with naivete, creating a many-headed Hydra of ignorance. One motorist crossing the US-Canada border asked Ivan Hiscocks, a border services officer who lives in Saint-Armand, Quebec, "Why don't you open more tollbooths?" When Randy Kearse is selling his self-published books on the subway, many subway riders will say "Can I see that?," and then take one of the books in hand. "They'll thumb through it, flip it, turn all the pages—on the street we call this finger-fucking. They'll finger-fuck the book, then hand it back to me!" Kearse explained, "Then the book looks tired."

Many park rangers view cell phones and their owners with alarm—callers on mountaintops have been known to request directions, guides, and refreshments; a few years back, a lost hiker in Jackson Hole, Wyoming, called a ranger requesting hot chocolate. Mannie Gentile, a park ranger who lives in Boonsboro, Maryland, says the proximity of his workplace to our nation's capital sometimes elicits high-powered name-dropping—and, on one occasion, a request from a member of Congress for "bellhop service." And I think we can all imagine the look of befuddlement on Gentile's face when one park visitor leveled him with that time-honored jewel, "Do you know *who* I am?"

But the great majority of requests in this category take the form of requests for free goods or services. Alice Shin of Kogi—Los Angeles's popular fleet of Korean

BBQ-To-Go trucks—said a typical request like this might run, "I love Kobi/Kojee's! I've been following Kobi/Kojee's forever! You guys are amazing and so wildly popular! So, I've got a movie premiere/band that's releasing an album/movie shoot—do you think you could park out there for six hours and donate food to the staff/fans?"

A variant here is an attempt at exchange: Birmingham, Alabama, resident Linda Gutowski said, "Early in my massage practice, I would sometimes have clients call about a gift certificate that they received, saying they didn't really want a massage, could they just have the cash?" (Gutowski's answer: No.)

The final category of rude question falls under the heading "Too Personal." To be sure, a lot of these interrogatory sallies are financial in nature. It is my fervent hope that Stephin Merritt, the Los Angeles–based singer-songwriter of the band the Magnetic Fields, will one day be recognized for being the Cole Porter of our day, but for now he must endure more earthbound irritations like the question "You make a lot of money with that?" And no self-respecting professional wants to hear the question that New York City private-practice psychotherapist Maggie Robbins sometimes does: "So are you basically supported by your husband?"

Sometimes the questions get even more personal. "Patients have no hesitation to comment about my weight," says Augusta, Georgia, physician Robert Lamberts. "I think that is because I weigh them each time they come in and so they feel entitled to turn the tables. One time I even had a person who had been my patient for a long time say, 'Whoa, Dr. Lamberts, you've put on a lot of weight! Are you pregnant?'"

This kind of question reaches its apogee with members of professions that require guns. C. J. Grisham, an army master sergeant in Temple, Texas, said, "The rudest question that someone can ask a soldier—or any combat veteran—is 'Have you killed anyone?' or 'How many people have you killed?' The unfortunate side effect of being in the military and sent to combat is that there may come a day where we are called to have to take the life of another man. It's something that weighs heavily in all our minds and is something we don't want to dwell on."

Grisham added, "I usually tell them I didn't kill anyone that didn't deserve it, but I'm willing to adjust my philosophy if they're willing to help me test it."

## Fantail Formation

I bought a pile of newspapers and magazines at the Newark airport the other day. I flopped the publications down onto the counter and fanned them into a peacock-tail configuration on the counter.

"That's so you can see everything I'm buying," I told the news vendor in the manner of a five-year-old boy who wants you to know that he's putting the *blue* cement truck on the edge of the rug so it won't get mixed up with the red one in the middle of the rug, let alone the blue tractors circling the coffee table, or any of the bendy Smurfs who resemble arthritic burros.

The vendor looked slightly baffled by my presentation. But ultimately he conceded, "I can see everything."

# V

*Being a brisk snowshoe across
the winterscape that is the Internet.*

It's called "inattentional blindness." That's the tag doctors and scientists have given to the state of monomaniacal obliviousness that overcomes you when you're wholly absorbed in an activity to the exclusion of other incoming data. Like when you're checking your e-mail or listening to an iPod, and don't notice that a deer has crept through your back door and is circling your coffee table, about to urinate on this week's issue of *Newsweek*.

Or when you log on to a laptop and forget that you're flying a plane. This actually happened (take note, Kent Wien of Boston, Massachusetts) in October 2009. Two Northwest pilots mistakenly flew 150 miles past Minneapolis because—they claimed—they were poring over the company's new flight-scheduling regulations. Stranger yet: Almost concurrently, researchers at Western Washington University announced to the world that when a clown on a unicycle pedaled through an open square on the university's campus, roughly 75 percent of passersby who were talking on cell phones failed to notice him. We have no hard data on the possible cross-pollination of these two events—i.e., whether the pilots would have noticed an airborne clown, or what the university crowd would have made of the Northwest plane had it buzzed the Western Washington squad one morning. And yet, a pattern emerges.

When we are drawn into a technological reality, we become inattentionally blind to the charms of unicycling clowns. We overshoot the airport runway. We exhibit shocking disregard for our newsweeklies. All of which of course holds dire implications for our manners.

Sometimes these technological realities hold sway even when their participants have been removed from the technological reality for half an hour or so. I told Dr. Ruth, "When I was single, I went through a period when partners would check their e-mail directly after sex."

Dr. Ruth responded, "Catastrophe!"

~⚬~

I'm always surprised by how often I leave a party or function with a slight feeling of failed intimacy or failed connection. Whether I meet someone in a close mutual friend's kitchen, or at a random event in a public space, people are often reluctant when I try to chat them up. They'll respond to a couple of my conversational prompts, but will offer few or none of their own. Next, I'll typically make a passing reference to my boyfriend, so that they know I'm not trying to hit on them. Often, I'll resort to asking them admittedly boring questions ("How do you know our hosts?" "Where do you live?"). If, after I've asked four of these, my interlocutor generates none of her own, I am led to believe that this person would rather be doing something other than talk to me, so I bid him or her adieu. Sometimes, if the person has been especially reluctant, I will self-flagellate a little—I'll walk away fearing that I've come off as a social climber or a preppy marm; or that they think I have extended, and then withdrawn, my sex tentacles.

Letitia Baldrige writes of a man at a barbecue who tried and tried to chat up the young woman seated next to him. "He asked her question after question, with one-word answers coming back. He told her about himself— his job, what he did in his leisure time—with practically no reaction. Finally he put his elbow on the table, rested his cheek in his hand, looked her gravely in the eyes, and said, 'I've told you everything about myself. I've asked you everything about yourself. Would you like to hear about my dog?'" At which point, the woman laughed, and the ice was finally broken.

Which is all to say: We Americans are not terrific at making conversation with people we don't know well.

So every time I hear about the advent of some groovy-sounding form of new media—be it MySpace or Twitter or Tumblr or Loopt or Cheek'd or any of the other assaults on orthography—it makes a kind of sense. We keep trying to invent new ways to talk to one another. Which speaks to a certain desire—a missed connection we're trying to fulfill.

## E-mail and the Lesser Angels

As noted earlier, some people decry the Internet as the beginning of the end. For them, this Wild West is just a little *too* wild.

This is the medium that gave birth to the charming bit of badinage that is *RTFM*—an acronym for "Read the F#*$&%! Manual." Frankly, when it comes to Internet etiquette, isn't it too easy to blame the medium and not its users? A historical view would suggest that, in most cases, the protestations of the technologically reluctant are ultimately a source of ridicule. In her 1987 book *When Old Technologies Were New: Thinking About Electric Communication in the Late Nineteenth Century*, Carolyn Marvin points out that many Victorian Americans were just as vexed by the telegraph and telephone as later generations would be by television and the Internet. In 1884, a Philadelphia newspaper's editor exhorted its readers "not to converse by phone with ill persons for fear of contracting contagious diseases." In a commonly told joke about the advent of the telephone, a caller's anxious "Are you there? Are you there?" finds a country bumpkin on the other end of the line silently and repeatedly nodding his head. (Early jokes about the telephone were *terribly* amusing.)

Or, I suppose, you can go back even farther in time, to when the chatty Socrates got his toga in a twist over the advent of written language based on an alphabet. Socrates thought scrolls would both erode memory and curb the back-and-forth exchange of ideas in real time.

The two main impediments to good online manners are the medium's incredible ease and its blankness of tone. On the former front, an e-mailer's ability easily to reach out to someone else without having to look that person in the eyes (let alone pick up the phone or address a letter or fashion puffs of smoke into recognizable code) can spur on impulsiveness. "The speed of e-mail doesn't just make it easier to lose our cool," Will Schwalbe and David Shipley write in their book *Send: The Essential Guide to E-mail for Office and Home*—"it actually eggs us on." The authors posit that people aren't quite themselves on e-mail, but are "angrier, less sympathetic, less aware, more easily wounded, even more gossipy and duplicitous." They conclude by noting how "e-mail has a tendency to encourage the lesser angels of our nature."

Indeed, not having to look into your interlocutor in the face frees you to write things you otherwise might not. Furthermore, "the Internet has no means to allow realtime feedback (other than rarely used two-way audio/video streams)," the psychologist Daniel Goleman notes. This "puts our inhibitory circuitry at a loss—there is no signal to monitor from the other person. This results in disinhibition—impulse unleashed." A bank robber doesn't just wear a mask because it protects his identity; it also helps him to tap into his ugly.

In some instances—or one, at least—all this tumult has led to something witty. In 1990, attorney and author Mike Godwin gave birth to Godwin's Law of Nazi Analogies when he observed, "As an online discussion grows longer, the probability of a comparison involving Nazis or Hitler approaches 100%."

But in most instances, the tumult has simply led to a lot of random bitchy comments. Consider the case of skateboarder Jake Brown. At the X Games in 2007, Brown fell about fifty feet to the ground when trying to land a two-spin rotation on a 293-foot half-pipe (called, appropriately enough, the Mega Ramp). When a video of this spectacular wipeout went up on YouTube, one person wrote in the comments section, "HIS SHOES POPPED OFF. LOL," while another posted, simply, "Ha ha ha ha ha ha." In June 2010, a Tennessee couple hiked to the top of a mountain where the young man was going to produce a ring and then propose to a girl; but before he did so, lightning struck and killed her. When the incident was posted on Facebook, 257 people hit the "Like" button.

Clearly, such people suffer from a kind of heartlessness; but what can those of us who don't suffer in this way learn from them? What does all this talk of blindness and disinhibition mean in practical terms for those of us who spend a large portion of our days staring at a screen? Primarily, I would venture, the lesson is that we should probably pay more heed when we hear that voice in our head that says, *Should I send this?*

There should be a word—a long, German one, no doubt—for e-mail's version of post-natal depression. Or maybe it's the aha moment's ugly cousin, the uh-oh moment. Whenever I send something that yields subsequent second-guessing, I am haunted by a statement made in a 2003 *New Yorker* article about people who survive jumping off the Golden Gate Bridge. One of the jumpers interviewed—Ken Baldwin, who, severely depressed, had tried to commit suicide at age 28—told writer Tad Friend that, upon hurling himself into the air, "I instantly realized that everything in my life that I thought was unfixable was totally fixable—except for having just jumped."

Certain kinds of messages are potential jumpers. They're better conveyed by forms of communication other than e-mail. Specifically, messages that are emotional; that announce your bold departure or change of orientation on a previously discussed matter; or that require a lot of feedback or negotiation. In all three instances, a discussion, either in person or by phone, is likely to prove a more successful communication because it allows for give-and-take.

You never want to bring a lion-size problem into a house full of LOL cats.

## Flatter than a Pancake

Which brings us to e-mail's second impediment to good manners: tone. The computer screen, while great for rendering so many things in riveting HD, has something of the glassy-eyed dead fish when it comes to written communication. This flatness of tone should come with its own eerie, synthesizer-heavy Angelo Badalamenti soundtrack. "I've never used so many exclamation points in my life!!!," I wrote to a friend in 1995 when we'd begun doing most of our corresponding online. She wrote back, "I know!! It's crazy!!!!!!"

The dead-fish effect is deepened in the case of the one-word response: Who among us has not written an impassioned, thousand-word e-mail to someone we admire, only to receive in return a response that runs, in toto, "Thanks"? Or, even worse, "thx"? I once garnered a "thx" in response to my having sent a fellow writer a long, admittedly rambling, rave about a magazine article he'd written. When my eyes beheld his threadbare "thx," they instantly widened. So, if only to amuse myself, I highlighted the thx and then enlarged its font size. Slightly better. Then I added *an* to it, to create *thanx*. Then I capitalized the *t*, re-spelled *thanks* correctly, added a comma and "Henry," and then garnished with an exclamation point! Hospitality is born.

Admittedly, e-mail is a poor cousin to other forms of communication when it comes to congratulations. While I like the idea that an e-mail allows the recipient of congratulation to decide whether to respond or not—particularly in the case of someone who is modest but who is currently plagued, darling, *plagued* with well-wishing—it lacks the heft and gravitas of a written note.

Look to the example of Abraham Lincoln. Though President Lincoln was so besotted with the telegraph that he would hunker down in the White House telegraph office for hours at a time, he knew when he needed to offer up something a little more artisanal. When General Grant captured Vicksburg, the commander in chief might have banged out a telegram for speedy delivery, as Tom Wheeler reminds us in *Mr. Lincoln's T-Mails: The Untold Story of How Abraham Lincoln Used the Telegraph to Win the Civil War.* But instead Lincoln took pen in hand and graced foolscap with the heartfelt tidings, "I now wish to make the personal acknowledgment that you were right, and I was wrong." Lincoln was wearing orthopedic shoes.

Sometimes e-mail's flatness of tone reaches its reductio

ad absurdum: no tone at all, and a subsequent lack of substance. I'm always surprised by how many e-mail exchanges with family and friends take on the quality of concurrent monologues, in fact. For instance, A will say, "We've traded in the Subaru for a PT Cruiser, Jeannie got accepted to the U of M, and Tim is staging his own version of *Iron Chef* out in the garage." Whereupon B writes back, "We're going to Tulum for a week so we hired Sarah's son Jonah to feed our turtles."

End of exchange. No response, no questions. It's like a duet sung in two keys by lead characters facing away from each other.

Was U of M Jeannie's first choice? Is Tim using a hot plate out in the garage, or are we talking tailpipe cookin'? Are Jonah and his deadbeat girlfriend going to erect a pop-up meth lab in B's house for the week? Are there really *no* questions worth asking here?

And while, yes, you could say that, prior to the invention of the telephone, communication was always a series of monologues, the fact remains that it would be startlingly easy for either A or B to hit "Reply" and say "Sounds good," or "When you hit Tulum don't miss Xelha!" or "Are you out of your mind—Jonah and your turtles? He killed three of our goldfish and both of our dogs."

But on the whole, they do not.

The hot potato has been passed, and where it lands, it remains.

## Business E-mail: The Stakes Are Raised

When it comes to business e-mail, the demons of impulsiveness and insensitivity to tone can be particularly ferocious: Both sender and recipient have more at stake than they do in their civilian lives.

In the following exchange of e-mails between two lawyers, published on the websites of ABC News and Massachusetts Lawyers Weekly, note how tone escalates the drama, and how a three-word-long response brings that drama to its climax (and actually inspired one of the e-mail writers to turn the correspondence over to the media).

From: Dianna Abdala
Sent: Friday, February 03, 2006 9:23 PM
To: William A. Korman
Subject: Thank you

Dear Attorney Korman,

At this time, I am writing to inform you that I will not be accepting your offer. After careful consideration, I have come to the conclusion that the pay you are offering would neither fulfill me nor support the lifestyle I am living in light of the work I would be doing for you. I have

decided instead to work for myself, and reap
100% of the benefits that I sow. Thank you for the
interviews.

Dianna L. Abdala, Esq.

———

From: William A. Korman
To: Dianna Abdala
Sent: Monday, February 06, 2006 12:15 PM
Subject: Re: Thank you

Dianna—Given that you had two interviews,
were offered and accepted the job (indeed, you had a
definite start date), I am surprised that you chose an
e-mail and a 9:30 PM voicemail message to convey
this information to me. It smacks of immaturity
and is quite unprofessional. Indeed, I did rely upon
your acceptance by ordering stationery and business
cards with your name, reformatting a computer and
setting up both internal and external e-mails for you
here at the office. While I do not quarrel with your
reasoning, I am extremely disappointed in the way
this has played out. I sincerely wish you the best of
luck in your future endeavors.

Will Korman

———

From: Dianna Abdala
To: William A. Korman

Sent: Monday, February 06, 2006 4:01 PM
Subject: Re: Thank you

A real lawyer would have put the contract into writing and not exercised any such reliance until he did so. Again, thank you.

From: William A. Korman
To: Dianna Abdala
Sent: Monday, February 06, 2006 4:18 PM
Subject: Re: Thank you

Thank you for your refresher course on contracts. This is not a bar exam question. You need to realize that this is a very small legal community, especially the criminal defense bar. Do you really want to start pissing off more experienced lawyers at this stage of your career?

From: Dianna Abdala
To: William A. Korman
Sent: Monday, February 06, 2006 4:29 PM
Subject: Re: Thank you

bla bla bla

I love this exchange as an example of tonal dysfunction because, ironically, until her final missive, Abdala says "Thank you" twice in each of her messages. And yet.

The breezy overconfidence of Abdala's first letter is worsened by the clipped quality of her second letter, which bottoms out with the outright hostility of her third. She needn't have started rolling this snowball down the hill in the first place: In her initial letter, she should merely have thanked Korman and his colleagues for their time and their offer. There's usually no need to explain the specific reason why you're turning down a job; but if you do provide one, you want to avoid striking a tone that is, as the British say, stroppy.

<hr />

The true devil's candy of business e-mail, of course, is forwarding. If the essential piece of information to be gleaned here is "Never send any message to a business e-mail address that you'd be embarrassed to have the whole company read," a helpful addendum would be, "...Or anyone else, for that matter." In 2001, the CEO of a Kansas City–based health care information technology firm called Cerner Corporation sent an angry e-mail to his managers about his employees' work habits. "As managers—you either do not know what your EMPLOYEES are doing; or YOU do not CARE...In either case, you have a problem and you will fix it or I will replace you." The message was forwarded all the way to Yahoo's message board, where Wall Street saw it and assumed that Cerner was in trouble. In the blink of an eye, the company's stock had dropped 29 percent. Over the course of three days, the stock price fell from about forty-four dollars a share to thirty-four.

The consequences of your own act of e-mail forwarding are not likely to be as dramatic. And yet, a few guidelines might deter potential upset. It's important to scroll through the entirety of an e-mail exchange before forwarding; the fatal words "Sheila is a slut" may be buried in the first of thirteen linked messages. Second, attachments are, for some of us at least, a pain in the neck; if you suspect any of your recipients are on BlackBerrys or other PDAs, it's helpful to write in your e-mail a précis of what's in the attachment in the body of the e-mail. Lastly, if you're adding cc'ed recipients to a group e-mail, be sure to explain who they are and why you've added them. It may be perfectly obvious to *you* who Mara Wanamaker is, but the rest of us can only assume that she is your pot dealer.

## Businessberried

The muscle-flexing so prevalent in business e-mail takes on a new dimension of swashbuckle when BlackBerrys or other PDAs are employed. To attend a business meeting where five or more executives slap their BlackBerrys down on the conference room table like tribal warriors bearing severed heads reminds one that humans didn't get to the top of the food chain by sitting around in their pajamas. If it's okay to take notes during a meeting, the thinking here goes, then it must by rights be okay to beaver away on a smart phone.

Indeed, it may; each community has its own politic on this matter, and those who are entering that community for the first time simply need to look at others' behavior for clues. (Josh Rabinowitz, the director of music at Grey Group in New York, told *The New York Times* in June 2009 that he uses his smart phone during meetings to trade jokes and ideas and "things you might not say out loud" because it sometimes adds to a meeting's "productive energy." I'm glad I don't have to make presentations in front of Mr. Rabinowitz, as I would be wholly rattled.) *Project Runway*'s Tim Gunn told me about the time he arrived early at a charity luncheon and saw that everyone in the room was staring down at his own lap. Gunn thought, "I didn't realize this charity had a religious affiliation."

As with a social, or non-business, occasion, too—it is neither Pollyanna nor emasculating to announce to a group "Excuse me, but due to extenuating circumstances, I'll be taking notes/sending updates/romantically involved with my BlackBerry during the meeting." The same goes for a doctor who is on call but who finds himself at a dinner party: "Please don't be offended if I check my messages or e-mail from time to time, but, even now, as we tuck into the alternately healthful and butter-soaked offerings contained within the breadbasket before us, people are dying." Disclaimers are not nothing.

## Face Time

It's difficult to write about Facebook, but not for the reason you think—i.e., that in five or ten years or minutes, it's possible that it will go the way of MySpace and eight-track tapes. Rather, this social networking site (which I visit every day) is a challenge to address because Facebook's obnoxiousness is not just inherent, it's intentional; Oscar Wilde would surely have loved Facebook. Many people use the site solely to promote themselves or their work; indeed, some posts are so auto-congratulatory that they practically self-lubricate. I had to de-friend myself from one writer whose book made many Best Book of the Year lists: each time the author posted a new Best of the Year list she'd made, she also clicked the "Like" button lest we be uncertain as to whether she found this turn of events gratifying. My advice to her would be the same as my advice as reality show contestants who are compelled to announce "I'm not here to make friends—I'm here to win": You don't need to tell us this, the statement is implied.

Some Facebook scriveners are pure monologists—they

use the site only to advertise their accolades or actions and in-store appearances, and to accept offers of friendship, but never to respond to others' updates (or, in some cases, to their friends' comments on their updates). These people use Facebook as a kind of Roach Motel. This methodology is particularly prevalent among performers and other creative folk, who confuse their friends list with their fan base. You need spend only a month or two on Facebook before encountering the eight saddest words in the English language: "Mark Ekmann has commented on his own photo."

My heart also goes out to infertile couples who are forced to witness—unless they choose to "hide" their friends' posts—the parade of baby pictures and sonograms that get trotted out on Facebook. "I know it's not meant to hurt, but you feel like you're getting kicked every time you see these," an occupational therapist and fertility patient named Diane Colling told *The Washington Post* last fall; another woman told the *Post* about the day her cousin's profile picture turned to a grainy sonogram: "I felt like I got punched in the gut." Kicked, punched: There's nothing cool or McLuhan-esque about these women's reactions.

Then there are those of us who use the site as a kind of floating cocktail party. Such an approach is hardly pitfall-free, either. Some people are not in the habit of posting on the "walls" (home pages) or updates of their close friends because they feel they are close enough not to need a social networking site to interact with them. So if someone close to you seems to be ignoring you, it's possible your friend feels a kinship with you that does not translate to Facebook. Even more likely, he probably has so many friends he just hasn't seen your updates. Or, third possibility, perhaps he just isn't inspired by the things you write on the site. Granted, it seems wholly unfair: There he is, deigning to comment on one of his friend's utterly galvanizing bombshells that she has wolfed down that totally delicious everything bagel, but he was unable even to hit the "Like" button for your tuna sandwich!

Is it rude if someone refuses to accept your friend request? If you've actually met in the flesh, then, yes, it sounds like it is. It's rude, too, in instances where you have not actually met, but have enjoyed a long period of correspondence or phone calls, or have heard about each other for years and years through mutual friends.

However, before we become offended, it's important to consider the snubber's Facebook modus operandi. Some people on Facebook only friend family or people they are offline friends with; others want to friend every single person they can possibly get their cyberpaws on. (I fall into the latter group. I enjoy randomly collecting themed groups of people. Among my collections: beautiful young Greek people; Greek people whose names are more than twenty characters long; and bearded members of the clergy.)

Sarah Thyre, a writer and performer who played the gym teacher on *Strangers with Candy* and wrote a memoir called *Dark at the Roots*, says she won't friend people she doesn't know because she often posts photos and videos of her kids. "I also don't accept friend requests from people with obvious fake names like Rusty Lickins or Clitty Jones or Knotty Crevasse because they will write all kinds of unfunny shit all over your page." As Thyre sees it, "They blew their wads on their pseudonyms."

Thus, in some cases, a person's failure to accept your friendship is less a response to you specifically than it is the result of an approach. Other people refuse friendship requests from people whom they don't specifically remember, which is why it's always best to send a message with your friendship request, so that your potential new friend is reminded that it's *you*—you know, the bubbly redhead from Graziela's brunch who said that the name *Real Simple* sounds like it's a magazine for people with learning disabilities.

Tagging, or posting photographs onto someone's page, is fraught, too. Lawsuits have been waged, hearts have been broken, and jobs have been lost over the appearance of incriminating information. Sending your friend a photo of that year in college when you dressed up as Eastern European trannies is, yes, a lovely gesture—but if you sent it to him privately via e-mail rather than publicly via his home page, you'd be giving him the authority to decide whether the world needs to see it. Ditto photos taken of him at recognizable, or identified, parties—are you sure that everyone who is going to see that picture was invited to that party?

Similarly, any written comments that fall under the categories of sex, religion, or medical crisis should probably be given a thorough once-over before being published—especially if your circle includes children, pious folk, or people with grave illnesses. (I exclude politics from this list because online political debate, though typically boring, is easily averted by the prickly.) Imagine the potential readers of your comments, and whether these people might reasonably take offense. Will the joy your lymphoma joke brings to twenty of its recipients merit the offense that it will bring to two others? (You may decide it does. I make no judgment here. I simply suggest you contemplate—in advance—the consequences of your actions.) Has anyone in the group recently lost someone to cancer? Consider.

Have you been unfriended? I have. It hurts. In one case, the reasoning was all too clear to me (an ex, whom I'd tried to re-befriend over dinner, but whom I'd instead subjected to three hours of psychological torture and heavy garlic.)

In other cases, though, I've had no clue. Had I offended this person? (If so, how? None of my bearded clergy were bothered!) Had I bored them? Had they closed their accounts? No clue. I certainly didn't expect, or particularly want, an explanatory e-mail from my ex; but in the instance of the person who is closing an account, I think it'd be thoughtful for him to send one last e-mail from the deck of the *Titanic*.

Ideally this "exit e-mail" would not make those remaining behind feel like total losers. Still, for some, the abrupt going-out-of-business is a proclamation of certain values. Not a rejection of all us friends, but of Facebook and its ethos. A writer of poetry, short fiction, and biography I know, an elegant lady soon to turn ninety-one years of age, has recently intimated that she has a pact with two mutual acquaintances: On her birthday, they'll meet—online, via Skype—for a martini, and commit simultaneous Facebook suicide.

Suicide announcements—whether virtual or otherwise—just aren't good manners at all.

Those social networking sites that are dating-oriented are, of course, particularly tension-filled. You can imagine the hurt feelings and neurosis that ensue when one Match.com person who's gone on six dates with a funny, fabulous Match.com person sees that said person's profile is still available for public view. Or when a particularly long and sloggy dinner conversation about the making of the *Lord of the Rings* trilogy inspires one JDate.com member, the next morning, to remove "Movies" from her list of interests.

Indeed, in the crowded barroom that is the Internet, sometimes we need to cut our losses. Thyre told me, "Recently a 'friend' I've known in real life for twenty years started writing 'clever,' mostly skeevily sexually suggestive comments after every single one of my posts. Stopping short of outright unfriending, I put a freeze on his ability to do so—you can block a person from posting. I should have known that this person, with his EST- and Landmark Forum–enhanced personality, would call me on it. And did I admit it? No! I blamed the freezing out on an imaginary hitch in the latest Facebook design and then said, 'A lot of my friends got frozen out and I'm just getting around to changing them back.' I lied to protect myself. Why? Because I've had enough psychotherapy to feel I deserve to lie occasionally. It's called 'boundary setting.'"

## Avatard

In an article he wrote for *The New York Times* in January 2009, David Carr said that "the ethos of Twitter, which is based on self-defining groups, is far more well-mannered than many parts of the Web—more Toastmasters than mosh pit." Carr's reasoning was that, when you tweet, you are your own avatar and your avatar is you, "so best not to act like a lout and when people want to flame you for something you said, they are responding to their own followers, not yours, so trolls quickly lose interest."

But it's also possible to be your own avatar *and* have bad manners. About 20 percent of the people who buy Loopt, a mobile tracking service that allows you to monitor friends' location via a GPS app on your cell phone, are one or both halves of a couple looking to keep tabs on the other half or each other. But as of 2010, Loopt's chief executive announced in January of that year, the company has seen a large increase in people who use Loopt to publicize fake locations as a decoy.

In an effort to get a taste of the avatar experience as it pertains to manners, I started buying clothes on a website called MyVirtualModel.com. You type in your measurements, weight, skin tone, face shape, hairstyle, and posture, whereupon an avatar who looks pretty much like you appears onscreen. Then you upload a photograph of your face onto the blank-looking default face, *et voilà*: a virtual Barbie, complete with Kenitalia. You use your avatar to try on and buy clothes from a variety of retailers, all from the safety of your own home or office—no standing in line, no anguishing about your refolding skills.

My experiences with my avatar are emblematic of online manners as a whole: I'm much more emotionally volatile as an avatar or avatar operator than I am as a human. But because my avataric experiences occur in an alternate dimension, they have less valence, and are more easily forgotten, than real-life experiences.

Admittedly, much of my irritation is about the technical aspects of the experience, rather than the experience itself, and thus can be classified as meta-irritation. But meta-irritation is no less potent or felt than irritation. I am reminded of the small child of a friend of a friend who, on leaving a 3-D screening of *Avatar*, said to his mother, "I wish there were 3-D in reality."

Mother: Reality *is* 3-D.

Child: So why don't the glasses work?

My first fit of pique came when I uploaded my face photo onto the avatar. I couldn't figure out how to size the photo properly, and my resultant big-headedness made me look like a doe-eyed waif from planet Black Velvet. "Screw this!" I yelled at my computer screen on my sixth attempt. I went to the site's bulletin board and posted a message titled "Can't get my face to stay on." A helpful webmaster gave me some instruction but my repeated efforts proved unfruitful. Ultimately I resigned myself to acromegaly, figuring if I went back to tech support and got the same guy, he'd just say, RTFM.

Then I discovered the "Rotate" function on MyVirtual-Model, which allows you to turn your avatar around for side and rear views, and suddenly I was asking a friend, "Does this head make my ass look big?" Seconds after I'd done so, I thought: Hmm, that's a slightly obnoxious question to ask out of the blue. Inattentional blindness?

Then when I e-mailed my avatar—dressed in various garments I was considering buying—to friends and family, one respondent betrayed her opinion that I wear my clothes too tight. (Hmm, I thought, that's a slightly obnoxious comment to get. Inattentional blindness!) Once again, a technological advance that seemed like it would draw me closer to other humans had in fact had the opposite effect.

Irritated by how easily both this respondent and I had become peevish, I took it out on my avatar: Using the website's scenery-changing option (you can position your online likeness in front of thirty locations, including a disco and a ballroom), I placed him, in his bare feet, against the snowy winterscape. Donner Party avatar.

A month later, I created a second avatar. A sidekick avatar. This one's the same height as me, and has my complexion and posture, but, at 350, weighs 190 pounds more than me. I call him Benny. Not many of the clothes on MyVirtualModel fit Benny, and his fleshy folds literally stretch the site's default garment—white briefs—to transparency.

But he looks a lot happier than me.

He can really make the disco background come alive.

# VI

*In which greetings and conversation are plumbed for their potential either to off-put or to butter.*

If the growth of new media coincides with an increasing inability to hold traditional, face-to-face conversations, it would seem to behoove us, at this point in the discussion, to address the sport of conversation.

I use the term *sport* rather than *art* because the ability to break the ice with strangers—and then to cling to that ice with a focus rivaled only by polar bears contemplating data on carbon emissions—is not God-given. It is a muscle. A muscle that can be strengthened by weight training.

But before we can start talking to people, we need to acknowledge that they are standing in front of us. This tends to be very easy if we're total strangers or close friends, but much more complicated if we're acquaintances; or if the relationship in question is a combination of professional and social; or if we find ourselves meeting in a battle zone, the foyer of a house of prostitution, or a drug den. Hug? Kiss? Kiss *à la européen*? Handshake with additional shoulder caress for added meaning? The possibilities dazzle.

The dictates of business environments, particularly corporate ones, tend to trump social ones, and often require nothing more than a handshake; look for clues such as constraint or recoiling. If you notice that everyone around you seems to have settled on the elbow bump as the local currency—as is sometimes the case in areas where the Ebola virus has erupted—then you'll want to be able to do this without awkwardness: Practice at home or in your accommodation, until it doesn't look like you are checking for underarm stains. Know, too, that it may take you a while to find your idiom, whatever that may be. I number among my acquaintances a tomboyish (white) woman from the suburbs who cringes at any form of physical intimacy; I spent months and months pecking her on the cheek before realizing that her preferred interaction is either no physical contact at all or, better yet, a soul-style fist bump. Sistah.

The widely accepted form of salutation in America between two women, or two urban gay males, or two members of the opposite sex whose bond is primarily social, is a quick peck on the cheek, or a brief hug. (Heterosexual males engage in hugging with one another, but generally on the gridiron, court, diamond, or soccer field, in the presence of millions of witnesses who are prepared to testify that there was nothing queer about the embrace; indeed, so flagrantly unhomosexual is this display of affection that it is sometimes accompanied by a healthy, red-blooded squeeze of the teammate's bum.) Additional earnestness or a separation of some months may prolong such hugging.

After initial impact, some people like to linger up close with you, laying their hands on your shoulders as they talk to you in a configuration I think of as "Dance Class." Men, other than as noted parenthetically, tend to want to shake hands or briefly to grab the shoulders of other men they see frequently. There are non-athletic male huggers, but they're the exception that proves the rule (and probably, we can be honest, have vague tendencies better left undiscussed); they're easily recognized by certain signs such as a goatee and/or employment in arts management. Humorist Colin Nissan's book *Don't Be That Guy* helps us sort out the confusion in all this subtext, giving a good idea of when a heterosexual man wants to be hugged by those who are neither going out with him nor paying down a mortgage with him—when he gets married or has a child, or when "I return from combat, someone dies, I earn a degree, I go into surgery." Nissan does not want to be hugged when "I spring for lunch, I get a hit in softball, I get over a cold, I get blackjack."

Living as I do in a glittering metropolis, I am faced with an unusual salutations-based quandary. As I explained to the openly gay Tim Gunn, "There are two groups of people in my life—the gays, and friends who have lived in Europe—who sometimes want to kiss me on the lips."

"Oh, dear!"

"Yes."

"No, no, no, no, no, no, no, no. Lips are for lovers. I do the both-cheeks thing. I'm appalled! I really am. Heidi's the exception," he said, referring to his co-host, Heidi Klum. "She's German and she knows this isn't going anywhere."

I do not want to kiss on the lips, unless I am engaged in a romantic relationship with you. So my friends and I do not kiss on the lips. The only awkwardness that has ensued has been with those friends with whom I have changed my stance—people with whom, out of a neurotic desire to prove that I did not crawl out of a box of Pepperidge Farm cookies—I *started* kissing on the lips, but stopped when I'd determined that lips are too eely. You should not change course midstream, unless a friendship has greatly deepened and you want to enhance or bump up your greeting. But even in these instances, beware potentially treacherous waters. Know that people will read all sorts of subtext into your divagations. Make sure they *want* to be licked.

In a 2006 op-ed in *The Boston Globe*, writer Dan

Akst, author of *We Have Met the Enemy: Self-Control in an Age of Excess*, posited that social kissing is a socially sanctioned system by which members of the opposite sex "build immunity toward one another." Believing that humans didn't evolve to spend extended periods of time in the company of members of the opposite sex whom they're not romantically involved with, Akst sees social kissing as "regulated infidelity," meant to inoculate against courtship. He points out that, although hugging and kissing as forms of greeting go back at least to the Old Testament, palling around between members of the opposite sex arose only in the 1920s when men and women started attending more mixed social functions; it symbolized the two sexes' ability to control themselves in each other's presence.

I'm uncertain whether I'm partial to Akst's theory because it's so clever or because, as a WASP, I endorse any measure that discourages intimacy with anyone other than unsuspecting waiters. But that's a conundrum for another day. The point is: Were everyone to operate under the "building immunity" principle—and I wish they would—the world would be host to far fewer salutation violations. We'd see, at one end of the spectrum, less standoffishness, and, at the other, less unnecessary lingering. We all might more naturally and organically arrive at a more or less standard operating procedure: a peck on the cheek and then back to our corners.

## Talking: How to Prepare for It

"Ideal conversation must be an exchange of thought," says Emily Post, in *Etiquette*, and "not, as many of those who worry most about their shortcomings believe, an eloquent exhibition of wit or oratory."

I agree—yet the chatty bore steals the spotlight of Post's hypothetical party, and also of this chapter of her book. My own experience suggests that the overly garrulous are, in fact, not conversation's chief nemesis—they can be gently interrupted, or given a bit of direction, or, worst-case scenario, abandoned.

The worst are those who refuse to engage or initiate or remark or ask. You can bring Muhammad down off the mountain, but you can't make the mountain say anything remotely interesting to Muhammad: It's a mountain. Rocks and stuff.

Conversational openers among strangers are, of course, highly challenging to formulate, and tend toward either the obvious ("How do you know Tim and Erica?" "How long have you worked for the company?") or the too-clever ("Which Food Network personality would you like to marry, and which would you like as your personal chef?"). I would ask that anyone who hears either variety try to be indulgent—those of us who tend to seize the reins of the conversation are trying our damnedest, and if you can just bear with us as we sputter to a start, we'll thank you mightily. Maybe, now and again, make it worth your trouble. Senators in ancient Rome hired people called nomenclators to follow them around and introduce them to people; sadly, most of us today are heavy with nomenclatorlessness.

We all have our MOs. I tend to ask a lot of questions, and then, ultimately, to become bored or irritated when my partner doesn't ask any back. But a series of questions isn't necessarily the best way to go—many people are made uncomfortable by the implied hot lights. Monologizing, too, is a perilous tack to take; as my brother, Fred, once prescribed, "Never give a thorough answer to 'How are you?'"

A smoother route to charmed interaction may be a statement about the room or situation in which you currently find yourselves. ("Is this *flocked* wallpaper? That word always sounds so dirty." "This is the first boat I've been on that hasn't capsized. Yet.") I remember one particularly beguiling opening salvo. After I had exchanged names with someone at a Christmas gathering in a crowded restaurant, she said to me, "Look at this, look at this!" and pointed to another guest who was brushing half a tray's worth of decorated cookies into a handbag, presumably her own. Mouths agape, my new acquaintance and I became immediate and lasting friends.

I love it when a stranger whom I've met at a gathering opens with an explanatory salvo: "I went to college with Rick, and both our kids play on the softball team, though my Sean *is just a little more talented than Rick Jr.*" Blammo: Suddenly I have acres of ground to cover with this person. I had a very lively conversation with the woman who walked up to me at a gathering once and said, "I've been kicked twice at this party." I was, of course, fairly desperate to know who at the gathering had kicked her; after she'd pointed out the culprits, we developed elaborate psychological profiles for those two guests.

I've long been a fan of the way in which older women will sometimes kick off a conversation with a preempt—when I interviewed sociologist Setsuko Nishi she told me, "I have benign hand tumors, so don't worry"; my mother likes to tell the person she's seated next to "I'm hard of hearing, so if any of my comments tonight seem absurdist, don't take it personally." So you can imagine how pleased I was to read a few years ago that Dolly Parton, when seeing a man become a little deer-in-the-headlights in the presence of Dolly and her awesomeness, will sometimes grab the man's head and pull it straight into her cleavage. Welcome to Dollywood.

It's important to be game and generous, especially if you're the one being chatted up. You may have nothing in common with the person you're talking to, but the fact is, you're here, and the other person who is attempting to start a conversation is simply being a good party guest. Help him out. As I alluded to earlier, one out of every eight strangers with whom I try to start a conversation at gatherings makes me feel like I'm trying to social-climb him or hit on him; whenever this becomes clear, I am led to wonder, How has civilization ever progressed? Yes, I ask too many questions. Yes, I walked over to you from the other side of the room because I saw you standing alone. But what if I'm walking around the room handing out five-hundred-dollar bills?

## Still Talking

It is neither nerdy nor calculating, particularly for those who are uncomfortable talking to strangers or acquaintances, to compile a list of possible conversation topics before you leave for a function. You may not end up resorting to any of them—but you will certainly feel more at ease. Moreover, this feeling of security may help you from blurting—one of the most common conversational pitfalls.

Blurting rarely showcases us at our best. It's easy when presented with a lot of new stimuli (or when you're in a rush or a vivid mood) to lose track of your tongue or manners, and meeting a new person brings you face-to-face with a lot of new stimuli. It can help, at any point before you arrive at the party, or meeting, or memorial service, or Tea Party rally, briefly to imagine each person whom you are likely to run into at the event, and what you might say to them. What was the last thing that you talked about with this person? Is there some long-in-the-making plot point in her personal narrative that you should ask about? Was she leaving for a trip or about to have collagen pumped into one of her extremities? If you can't remember, you can ask someone who might.

Because tone and facial expression are such powerful elements of conversation, able as they are to transform the most bland-seeming or libelous-seeming comment into high wit, it's difficult to refer to generic topics or statements that should be avoided when speaking to strangers. And yet, certain gambits—outside the commonly cited areas of religion and politics (and, in the presence of children, sexytime)—have a higher fatality rate than others. I refer to jokes, however gentle, about your fellow speaker's clothing; comments about what famous person they most resemble; comments about severe medical conditions; or the statement—when not followed by gentle buttressing or other follow-up—"You cut your hair."

I have several friends who are neither name-droppers nor social climbers but who, upon meeting someone new, love to trot out a list of names for a round of "Do You Know? Do You Know?" My friends' intention here is to establish intimacy and/or to make the world seem small. But some people are put off by being quizzed on the *Tulane Alumni Bulletin* or *Who's Who in the World of NGOs*. Maybe save Who Do We Have in Common? for the *second* date.

If you're eating food that someone present has

prepared, it can sometimes be rude to talk about food other than that which you're eating. Telling everyone about the amazing peach cobbler you had at the state fair last spring somehow makes the blueberry cobbler directly in front of you seem...lesser than.

As for topics likely to bring a bit of color to the cheeks, I admire people who casually warn, at the introduction of such points of conversation, "I have somewhat controversial feelings on the topic," or "Shana and I have a very long history." This kind of warning allows its hearer to decide whether to pivot or plunge.

## Complimenting Someone Other Than Yourself

Prominent in the good conversationalist's bag of tricks is the ability to compliment others. I would never encourage anyone to offer *false* flattery, except when dealing with the pathologically narcissistic or manifestly suicidal. In either of those cases, get as quickly as possible to mentioning that terrific psychopharmacologist you've been seeing. Usually, however, there is *something* to praise or approve of in others; to do so is to send a smoke signal that says *Your charms have not fallen on blind eyes nor on deaf ears.*

One of the paradoxes of good manners is that the actions of a very, very thoughtful person and those of a very skilled social climber are virtually identical: asking you about your ailing mother, wondering whether you are warm enough in that itty-bitty little sweater. And yet, when the chips are down, we know who's who.

Most people prefer to be complimented on something they've done (painted a room, closed a deal, raised a child) rather than on something they are (beautiful, adventurous, smart, scrupulous). A compliment wants to be specific, but not so specific that it's hair-splitting and seems calculated. If you tell a friend you love her new haircut, she'll probably smile; but if you tell her instead that you love the way her hair now curls around her ear when she's standing in a strong wind, she may start. She will spend more time than she ought to thinking about this comment. Too many compliments (or too strong a compliment) is just as bad as no compliment; one rarely wants to verbally fellate. Maybe the analogy to employ here is flowers: Compliments should be a single sunflower set on a windowsill for her to walk up to and admire, not three dozen roses delivered by an exhausted-looking bike messenger in an angel costume.

Memory has an interesting connection to manners. Recently, at a party I hosted, a gentleman invitee asked me whether, on the three dates that we'd gone on together six years prior, we had "fooled around."

Now, I grant you: Old age is very, very taxing (this gentleman is forty-five). The memory banks start to cloud, or to be covered with a caramel-colored, resinous sludge that is the mother of earwax. Events intermingle in our minds, either erasing themselves or cross-pollinating into freakish, double-headed crossbreeds. That new movie star fell asleep during a UN address! The president of Guyana had a rib removed to make his figure more boyish! Etc.

I'd like to think that my own modest skills as a purveyor of eros might have imprinted themselves on this fellow's mind with enough force to at least render their existence, if not the details of their application in this case, memorable.

But, no.

You may have been the recipient of a similar kind of query. A comment in the vein of "I think I just saw/read/heard/ate something that you created/wrote/composed/cooked." When our "appreciators" express acknowledgment in these vague terms, they do themselves no favors. What many of us hear in this statement is "Your building/article/song/meal did not make enough of an impression for me to remember it."

Compliments should be genuine but not so bland as to make no impression. It might behoove you to get into the habit, when experiencing things you may later have to summon up in a compliment, of latching on to a single detail—e.g., "That redwood chair in the lobby!" "I always love a perfect-bound project report much more than one in a ring binder."

Easier yet, you might have recourse to artfully specific blanket statements. "Every time I hear a piece of your music, I think of one of those small, zinc-topped café tables." Or, "Dude, your PowerPoint presentations rock!" "I read your Profit/Loss reports aloud to my children at bedtime."

A third alternative: Say nothing. Many of us would happily forgo distracted vagueness in favor of a rich, meaning-laden silence.

A similar landmine, of course, is "Have we met?" When I asked Judith Martin what she thought of this question, she said, "There are famous instances of people responding, 'Yes, we used to be married.'"

"One of Zsa Zsa Gabor's nine husbands said that to her once," I said.

"Someone told me there was a Nobel Prize winner, too. Someone congratulated him, 'I'm so glad! I always knew you could do it!' and he said, 'Do I know you from somewhere?' and she said, 'Yes, I'm your first wife.' So it can be dangerous. You have to have a really good memory to say that."

I've even been told, discreetly, names withheld, of a woman in her thirties, the offspring of Hollywood royalty, who attended a play in which a male relative was acting. After the show, an older woman approached the actor with congratulations, saying to him, "And who is this enchanting creature?" The enchanting creature in question was the older woman's own daughter.

If you cannot remember whether or not you have in fact met, then ask yourself, Does it really matter? Nine out of ten times, it doesn't. And nine out of ten times, you can figure out a way to say hello that is heartfelt and energetic enough to apply to either a person you've met or a person you haven't met. And it's always better to say "I know we've met, of course, but forgive me and my Alzheimer's...tell me your name again?"

Now if you can't remember whether you've fooled around with the person in question, perhaps it's best to stymie the impulse to divulge this information, and then to arrange your face in the manner of a seraphic Buddha.

Or: Wait until you have something wonderful to say about how you'll never forget the night I kissed you on your couch and told you that you were gorgeous.

## Self-Deprecation and Its Exhaustions

A little self-deprecation is a beautiful thing—but too much is not. A passing remark about your weight problem, or adorable alcoholism, may endear others to you. But the frequent repetition of same is more likely to cause mild panic. When given too private a view of the volcano's molten core, many hikers head back to the lodge. Those of us who like to self-lacerate need to keep tabs on what we're dishing out; a good rule of thumb is never to make your own problems someone else's.

I'm reminded of an (initially) charmingly neurotic gentleman I fell into conversation with at a party some years ago. When he told me, "I can't talk on the phone if other people are in the room," I chuckled in recognition, remembering the years I worked in open-seating-based offices: I discouraged friends from telephoning me at these places, because my awkwardness and whispering made me sound like I was about to tell them I had cancer. Then when the gentleman told me that he can't get a full night's sleep if someone else is in his bed, I thought, Unh-huh, a pattern emerges. But then, some minutes later, when he told me that he can't eat when others are in the room with him, I quickly started devising my exit strategy. What had originally seemed harmless shtick had metamorphosed into full-blown psychosis. Was he about to implode? And surely *I* was making him uncomfortable, too?

With the proper timing, the kamikaze self-deprecator can ratchet up his potential reign of destruction. Tim Gunn told me about the time he and his *Project Runway* colleague Nina Garcia went on Larry King's show. "As the producer was counting down—'Forty seconds, Larry!,' 'Thirty seconds, Larry!,' 'Fifteen seconds, Larry!'—Larry turned to us and said, 'By the way, I've never watched your show.'" Shaking his head at me in befuddlement, Gunn added, "'By the way'! Wow."

In its lower forms, self-deprecation is sometimes mere fishing for compliments, or a bid for reassurance. And at its absolute lowest, self-deprecation is basically bragging. Once a fellow author once told me that he is so prone to stage fright that he had to take sleeping pills *every single night* of his book tour through Europe. (Rotterdam: So noisy! The thudding of beer steins onto countertops so often induces migraine! ) I'm similarly nonplussed when people tell me how, due to their own crippling shortcomings or inadequacies or laziness or deadly hipness, they've turned down job offers and dinner dates—job offers and dinner dates that the rest of us would kill for.

A final stratum of self-deprecation carries the odor of insult. "I love your pants," I'll say to someone. At which point she offers, "These are the ugliest pants in the world." Skillful, how a compliment can be insta-flected as an insult to both parties.

## Evaluation without Litigation

Giving criticism to people you care about is, for some of us, the Olympics of manners: At conversation's end, we are sweat-soaked and spent, and need to spend the next few days in total isolation, rinsing out our unmentionables in a bathroom sink. This is true even in those situations—e.g., a classroom, or during a performance review at a job—when criticism would seem to be the very point.

In order to get a purchase on this very slippery piece of fish, I asked Tim Gunn out to lunch. Gunn's empathetic but wholly pragmatic evaluations of young designers' work on *Project Runway* have always struck me as being admirably balanced; Tim strikes with a velvet hammer. His twenty-five years spent teaching at Parsons School for Design has no doubt helped him in this regard. Moreover, when you read his book, *Gunn's Golden Rules*, you come away assured that this is someone who has spent a lot of time thinking about manners.

We met at the Bryant Park Grill, the restaurant immediately behind the New York Public Library. I'd love to tell you that Gunn showed up in a wife-beater and ripped jeans. But, no, Gunn wore pretty much exactly what you figure he did—a dark three-piece suit—and responded to my late-in-the-game seating request with nimble aplomb.

I ordered a chef's salad; when Gunn asked, "Do you want that chopped? It can be hard to eat," the rhetorical tone his inquiry struck made me realize that it didn't matter how I answered this question.

"Sometimes people who meet me for the first time say, 'I didn't know what to wear,'" Gunn told me. "And I always say, I would never *dream* of talking about what you're wearing unless you asked me to. At which point I would ask a lot of questions about you. I need to know things about you. It's a Socratic approach."

So for Gunn, the first step when giving criticism is knowing who you're criticizing. You wouldn't talk to your nephew, a freshman at CalArts, the same way you'd talk to Andy Warhol.

Gunn continued, "What used to happen a lot is that

someone would present me with the portfolios of two high school students, and ask me which was better. And I would say, I need to know who these two people are. What kind of background do they have, how are their grades? You may have someone who has great technical abilities and some kind of compelling vision versus someone who has a technically proficient portfolio and has been in a magnet high school for the arts. I want to know what opportunities they've been presented, and how they've used them."

Once Gunn knows the person he's talking to, then he wants to know what it is that the creator is trying to create. To you and me, that heavily distressed black Lycra tube is raring for a kick-ass night of rock and roll; but if the designer is trying to create an elegant cocktail dress, then something's amiss.

"If you've watched *Project Runway*, you'll know that the first thing I always say to designers is, Talk to me. What are you doing? What's going on? What are you trying to achieve?"

Then: "I think it's important to talk only about things that you can change. If a designer has a whole worktable full of black fabric, then I don't say, Gee, I wish you'd bought red fabric. Then I try to prioritize what my concerns are. I see how the designer responds to my larger concerns. If we're in agreement about the problems, then they see that I've tried to internalize what they're trying to do with the design."

Gunn's signature phrase "Make it work!" is germane here. He told me, "I don't really care whether you 'like' your design or not. I want to know whether it's working or not, and how it can be made to work better. *Like* and *dislike*—I don't want to sound disrespectful of either of those words, but they don't get you anywhere."

Gunn's pedagogical approach is clearly well honed— refined over many hours spent in the classroom-studio, and polished by a good deal of trial and error. But what about more run-of-the-mill situations? Does Gunn see fit to address tiny matters of style? Tucking delicately into my last bite of chef's salad—chopped to a fare-thee-well— I asked him, "Would you ever remove a conspicious cat hair from someone's clothing?"

"I do it all the time! Because I would want someone to do it for me."

"Would you tell someone he has spinach on his teeth?"

"If we're going on camera, yes."

"But what if, say, you were having a meeting as the chief creative officer of Claiborne Inc. with the head buyer at Macy's?"

"Can I tell you something? Buyers are such awful appalling people that I would revel in their having cat hair on them."

"You'd put *more* cat hair on them."

"Yes."

I suggested that unsolicited criticism is a particularly

complicated matter in New York City, where people will sometimes break the ice with strangers by kvetching.

"A friend and I went to an Off-Broadway play recently," I told him, "and as everyone was getting up at intermission to go into the lobby, the woman seated directly behind me said to me, 'Isn't this show *awful*?' And I said awkwardly, 'Uh, my friend here bought the tickets for my birthday.'"

"Or there's also 'My friend *wrote* the play.'"

"Exactly."

"It's like New York Tourette's."

"On the one hand, it's lovely that strangers want to talk to you..."

"But there's also the question 'What did you think of the play?'"

# VII

*Being an examination of the subset of manners known as protocol, with an emphasis on the ways we can deduce the parameters of this same subset, whenever we find ourselves in new, subset-heavy situations.*

...Some years ago, a human welfare organization employee was working in the West African country of Togo. After purchasing some beautiful beads one day, she wore them to a party that was being held upcountry. When she swanned into the party, she encountered moderate awkwardness: Locally, such beads are worn not as a necklace, but as part of a belt that holds up a kind of loincloth. In short, the woman had come to the party proudly wearing around her neck something that all the Togolese guests recognized as underwear...

...A gentleman who worked for a science museum in South Bend, Indiana, once greeted a busload of developmentally disabled children and their minders, who'd all come to the museum for a visit. While helping a member of the group named Amy to make an ID badge on one of the science center's computers, the museum employee became increasingly impressed by the ease and sophistication that Amy showed filling out the online questionnaire. He started reading the questions aloud to her, whereupon Amy, shrinking into her chair, told him, "I can read!" When the developmentally disabled kids' teacher walked over to the computer, the museum employee marveled to her, "Amy was just telling me that she can read." At which point the teacher explained to him that *of course* Amy could read—Amy wasn't one of the developmentally disabled kids, but one of the kid's older sister and minder...

...At a party in Ascot, England, thrown in 1983 in honor of the American businessman Jack Heinz, Princess Margaret asked Queen Elizabeth how she was enjoying herself. Alluding to the fact that the American guests at the party either didn't know or didn't care that the sovereign is not meant to be touched (men should nod, women should curtsy), the queen ruefully reported, "We have shaken many hands."...

Most good manners are, if not universal, at least international. But certain pockets of the world have their own mores—as we can see in the aforementioned three examples, which come respectively from the book *Do's and Taboos Around the World*; the radio show *This American Life*; and Gore Vidal's *Point to Point Navigation*.

It's not always clear what the particularities of these

site-specific or situation-specific mores are; sometimes we have to put on our deerstalker hat and invoke our powers of deduction.

We're now in the realm of protocol.

## Stranger in a Strange Land

At this point in our narrative, I'd like to look at how some individual circumstances and places can breed their own sets of expectations and rules. Because I am sometimes rattled when I encounter such areas of gray—don't get me started on my stay at an urban bed-and-breakfast where my host's vagueness about whether or not I could sit in her living room caused me to rearrange all the furniture in her guest bedroom as an act of revenge—I'll try here to offer some prescriptive measures about sussing out new situations lest you, too, be tempted to drag the immense oak bureau over by the window, pulling your back out in the process.

My friend Leslie was doing some cat-sitting in Ann Arbor one month a few years ago. Because the cat owner was a friend whom Leslie was helping out, some of the arrangements had been left a little vague. Yes, Leslie knew when to come to the house, and what to feed her little charges. But she wasn't sure what the additional benefits were. What if, say, Leslie—who was living at the time in a down-at-heel one-bedroom—wanted to spend an afternoon working on the cat owner's gracious patio; was that allowable? And was Leslie allowed to snarfle down any of the diverse and copious snack items in the pantry? Neither question seemed pressing enough to warrant sending an e-mail to the cat owner, who was holed up at an eighteenth-century agriturismo in Puglia for a much-needed retreat, and who would look upon such correspondence with the mild alarm of the hotel guest who has found a dead mouse in her bubble bath. Moreover, the cat owner was a friend of Leslie's—someone with whom Leslie liked to think she shared values and sensibility. To get in touch with the cat owner would be to somehow doubt or question the bonds of affection between the two women; Leslie felt like she ought to have an innate sense of her boundaries.

After about a week of devoted cat care and personal restraint, Leslie decided to forgo sitting on the patio—mostly because the cats pressing their noses against the glass of the sliding door would have proven too distracting to work.

But the snacking front proved more complicated. "I thought my cat-sitting duties had earned me *some* pantry-grazing," Leslie told me—but not a scorched-earth policy that left emptied jars of macadamia nuts bruised and panting from exhaustive pillaging. No, after furtively pawing through the cupboard for treasures—half a box of golden raisins, a pristine package of Pepperidge Farm Mint Milanos, a panoply of nuts, a spray of graham crackers in the shape of bears, and several half-filled plastic containers of some kind of Whole Foods–ish ancient grains—Leslie finally settled on an ethic: If the food item's container was already opened, she was allowed to eat it, as long as she left at least a portion's worth behind. And if the container was already opened but contained less than a portion, Leslie was allowed not only to eat the contents but also, yes, to feel slightly virtuous doing so. Cat-sitter *and* housecleaner. It worked out swimmingly—and Leslie and her host remain friends to this day.

Life is constantly presenting us with these kinds of contests or riddles. You're given a few details but no parameters—or a lot of parameters but no details—and then you're told, *Go!*

So you go.

But all along you wonder: Were those Teddy Grahams really mine to eat? Did I settle on the right protocol? All is uncertain. It's so much easier when you're handed a typed sheet by a natural blonde with the State Department in sweater set and pearls.

And if you've got any social mobility, and count among your acquaintance people from a variety of walks of life—as urban Americans increasingly do—you will often come back to a more vexing question yet: Is so-and-so (who's decidedly closer in station to me than Elizabeth II) entitled to expect the rest of us to observe protocol? Or is she getting a bit above herself?

That's the question around which protocol plummets

vertiginously down through manners, back to the plane of etiquette, even to the lower reaches of questionable style. An acquaintance who spent the go-go 1980s and early Clinton years as a New York City decorator related meeting his client—the wife of an American plutocrat, a very wealthy person, yes, but neither she nor her spouse-patron were royalty or high-ranking prelates—for a day of fabric shopping. He greeted her with a raise of his hand. But did so—gasp!—in front of the woman's *driver*! Whereupon he was coolly asked not to "wave at me in front of a member of staff; it's *just not protocol*."

Kind of makes you want to gobble all the cashew brittle and Snackwell's in her cupboard, doesn't it? And leave the sticky wrappers on the couch in her TV room.

But if you want to keep your job—and I'm assuming most of us do—then it helps to know that protocol can sometimes be very similar to an opera diva: highly arbitrary, difficult to parse, and subject to change without notice.

## Don't Sit Over Here

We Americans are not famous for our ability to understand, or coalesce with, other cultures, let alone their protocols—an area generally alien to us. Never show the soles of your feet or your shoes to a member of the Thai royal family. "I wasn't even considering it!" you want to say. But you might also have a follow-up question: Why not? Have Their Serene Majesties been kept in the dark for generations about the ugly fact that we commoners get around by walking?

America, unbudging. Perhaps it's only fitting that a country that takes exaggerated, sometimes extreme, pride in a "democratic" approach—and is bordered on two sides by ocean rather than by other peoples—would spawn a populace that is defiantly just-plain-folks and highly ethnocentric. In *The Ugly American*, the 1958 political novel by Eugene Burdick and William Lederer whose title has become a term for the kind of person who makes you cringe while on vacation—even though, it should be noted, the Ugly American in the book is the good guy—a Burmese journalist says, "For some reason, the [American] people I meet in my country are not the same as the ones I knew in the United States. A mysterious change seems to come over Americans when they go to a foreign land. They isolate themselves socially. They live pretentiously. They're loud and ostentatious."

In the same way that traveling the dark wilds of the Internet can unleash our insecurities and lapses in decorum, so, too, does traveling to Paris cause some of us to scream across a crowded café, "They're showing *American Idol* on the TV in the kitchen!" The unfamiliar induces a loss, or questioning, of our identity; in an effort to reestablish this identity, we sometimes overcompensate. Nowhere, it seems, is this urge less resistible than in situations in which we're called upon to observe a rarefied foreign protocol. There's something quintessentially American in the joke about the Texan who dines with an English duchess and two of her countrymen. During their meal, the lady experiences momentary gastrointestinal embarrassment—in the polite version of the story, "Her tummy rumbles." One of the English gentlemen immediately says, "Oh, excuse me." Her tummy presently rumbles again. The other English gentleman jumps in with, "Terribly sorry, wot!" When her tummy rumbles yet once more, the Texan generously says, "Have that one on me, ma'am."

Yet we observe protocol pretty easily when there's not an attendant language, culture, or class-system barrier. And you don't need to leave the country or the tangible world in order to find yourself in new territory. Anytime you start working at a new company, frequent an unusual milieu, or interact with people whose lives are changing dramatically, you may start to notice that the people around you are behaving in somewhat unusual ways. Your antennae start to thrum. Questions emerge. Why didn't Bob the bartender yell "Heeeeeeeeey Aaaaaaaaaaaaaaaart!," as he always does to his regular Arthur Ginblossom, when Arthur walked into the bar with a guy that no one had ever seen him with before? (Because Bob, attuned to the protocols of his position, thought Arthur might be on a job interview or having a glass of soda water with a prospective in-law.) How come no one at the law firm ever asks Arabella about her home life? (Because Arabella has said that her husband is employed in the waste management industries.) Why doesn't one of the organizers of the yoga seminar fix the goddamn coffee machine for once? (Because the seminar is underwritten by Stash Tea.)

The more practice you get at breaking the code, the better at it you get. I asked the Bronx-bred Bruce George, who co-edited the anthology of gang members' writing *Bandana Republic*, how having been in various street gangs—notorious bastions of hierarchy and custom—had changed the way he sees the world, and he said that he now notices a pecking order even when he gets on a subway or train. "The people who are already on the train—they have a certain comfort level about having already been on the train. They look at the new people and think, 'Don't sit over *here*!'"

## I, Spy

On entering new situations, there are a number of ways to help us potentially avoid awkwardness and embarrassment. For starters, we probably want to be careful of making assumptions. In the etiquette world, perhaps the most famous example of the perils of assumption is that of Mrs. Astor and the Vanderbilt ball. In March 1883, the arriviste Alva Vanderbilt planned to unseat, or at least jostle the seat of, the redoubtable Caroline Schermerhorn Astor as the doyenne of New York society. Mrs. Vanderbilt's weapon of choice was a ball that would make all previous New York balls look like feedlots. Exotic foods. Costumed guests. A tropical forest. At the quarter-of-a-million-dollar Vanderbilt shindig, a giant gondola would roll into the ballroom to distribute the evening's party favors—silver lockets and Tiffany bracelets.

Mrs. Astor assumed that an invitation would be proffered to her; indeed, it's said that, in the weeks before the ball, she even doubled up on dance lessons for her marriageable daughter, Carrie. After all, "Mrs. Astor was Old Blood royalty at its most incontestable moment," as Laura Claridge writes in her biography *Emily Post*. "It was no secret that the Astors looked down on the Vanderbilts, whose riches came from mere trade...The Astors had dirtied their hands the right way, trading pelts and selling pianos so long ago that no one remembered their past as merchants."

But...then...no...invitation...came. Mrs. A whipped off a slightly icy letter to Mrs. V, inquiring about her lost invitation; whereupon Mrs. V wrote back to say that, no, the invitation had not been lost, it simply hadn't been sent. Mrs. Vanderbilt explained that Mrs. Astor had never "dropped her card" at 660 Fifth Avenue—that is, left a "pasteboard," or calling card, at the Vanderbilt residence—and Mrs. Vanderbilt would never be so uncouth as to invite to her ball someone who'd never paid a call at her home.

Mrs. Astor smoldered and fumed for several days—a volcano in a tight-fitting bodice—before finally capitulating and sending to 660 Fifth footmen with a calling card to be given to the footman at the Vanderbilt gates. On being handed the card, "The victor purportedly bestowed a wicked smile of thanks upon her servant," Claridge writes. Mrs. Vanderbilt sent off an invitation to Mrs. Astor before the end of the day.

If we make assumptions about a new situation—particularly, it seems, assumptions that flatter us—then we set ourselves up for potential humiliation. Then we fail, or are slow, to take on the second course of action.

The second course of action I recommend to those who are entering new situations is to do some research. Do you have a friend who used to work at the company where you've just been hired—someone who might fill you in on the fascinating mores surrounding the office's sole bathroom key? Would a talk with your grandparent's nurses' aide or a medical professional help you with some of the more delicate matters related to taking care of an ailing spinster? Treat the new situation like another country.

If you're in fact traveling to another country, it's easy to buy a guidebook, of course, or to get Googly. But talking to someone who lives, or has lived, in the land you're about to visit might be even better. It's entirely possible to pore over travel guides to England and somehow overlook the fact that you're supposed to tip in restaurants there, but are considered a piker if you tip in pubs. Neither of my two guidebooks for Cairo told me to take only the city's white cabs, which unlike the black cabs have meters. And I wish some Francophone had alerted me to the whole *baiser/le baiser* thing.

Judith Martin told me, "Sometimes you need a mentor. I was looking for books once on courtroom etiquette. Courtroom etiquette is extremely strict. I was at a library here in Washington, and at the law library in Cambridge, and there was almost nothing. I realized it's because older lawyers train the younger lawyers. It's passed on that way. Just as, in an ideal society, nobody needs Miss Manners, they would learn from their parents and the people around them. So you watch and see what you can learn."

Indeed, once you've arrived at your new job site or social interaction or country, the best course of action is to be discreet and to be a keen observer. This should yield treasures. If you're in Japan on business, maybe you'll suddenly realize why your more-seasoned-traveler colleague had knowingly told you to be extra sure that your shoes were polished well for your trip (the Japanese— uncomfortable with too much direct eye contact, as stated before—go out of their way to employ humble body language, and tend to train their line of vision downward). Or maybe you'll notice that all the other parents who bring their toddlers to this particular tiny park on weekend afternoons seem to conduct rushed and highly abbreviated conversations (there's a magisterially silent Tai Chi class for seniors that meets at three PM).

Lastly, the person who finds herself plonked down in a new world should be unembarrassed about asking delicately phrased questions. "Excuse me, sir. I'm so sorry to bother you, but I've noticed that various places of worship around the world have differing traditions or rules about the covering of the head. This temple here—is it a hats-on or a hats-off kind of place?" Ask this question, and you are sure to be given a Notre-Dame de Paris gimme cap.

## Swap Till You Drop

In the end, though, I suppose the most important thing to be said about protocol is that ideally it is superseded by something more human. Once you master the ravines and ridges, you open yourself to the clouds—something I found out when I became a plant and shrub man.

My first memory here is of taking the F train all the way out to a neighborhood in Brooklyn called Windsor Terrace—about a forty-five-minute trip from Manhattan—while carrying two ten-inch-tall pepper plants. I'd corresponded with a guy I'll call Sander on VeggieTrader.com, a now-defunct website devoted to plant exchange—think Craigslist for herbs and vegetables.

I was going to unload my two peppers on him in exchange for two Roma tomato seedlings.

The thing was, though, Sander and I had never met or spoken, so instead of giving me his address, he'd only given me his cell phone number and the name of his subway stop.

When I got to the subway stop, I called. Sander had a low-pitched, slightly tentative sound. "What you want to do," he started, and then proceeded to give me directions that would take me about ten minutes to walk. At that point, he said I should phone again, and he'd give me his address. I wondered, Is this much cautiousness totally necessary?

Vaguely irritated, I walked and then phoned again.

"Great," Sander said. Now if I were to just keep walking down the street that I was on, he continued, I'd find a bodega across from a schoolyard. Sander lived right there, he said—in the red-brick building. So when I reached the red-brick building, all I needed to do was...call him again and he'd give me his apartment number.

Another phone call and another walk later, Sander, a bearded musician in his thirties, opened his door and saw me anxiously bearing two pepper plants. I told him, "I feel like a parent arranging a playdate."

We exchanged self-conscious hellos and he suggested we walk the fifteen feet out to his backyard to see his tomato plants.

I stymied my impulse to ask if he wanted me to go out in the backyard first, and then call when I got there.

## Chlorophilanthropy

I'd heard about VeggieTrader.com a few months earlier in a foodie newsletter that I subscribe to. "If you have too many tomatoes, and I have too many strawberries, it's a shame to let all that good food go to waste," the site's founder explained on the home page. It took roughly four seconds to join, and was free.

The nine advertisements that had been placed on the site by my fellow New Yorkers were sober affairs, and were heavy on tomato seedlings and mint, so I decided that the more I played up my own plants' exoticism, the more VeggieTrader action I would see.

With this in mind, I posted an ad for my twenty-inch-long vert petit de Paris cornichon vine, extolling its five blossoms, and its readiness to *"mobiliser, mon ami."* In an ad about my Masai filet bean plants, I mentioned that, like their tribal namesakes, they were "tall, regal music lovers." Of my Hungarian black hot pepper plants, I said, "Exotic, delicious, Carpathian: the Béla Bartók of veggies." Don't let the small leaves of my Greek basil fool you, I cautioned, their spiciness will make your pesto "erupt in a frenzy of bouzouki-based sound!"

On scrolling through my completed ads, my mind had recourse to the word *flashy*. Was I grandstanding here? I scrolled through the ads again and assessed their show-offiness. While my sin would more likely fall under the heading of Style as opposed to Manners, I didn't want to be ostracized by this new community either way.

I decided that, since my ads trafficked exclusively in the truth—a frothy, jazzercised truth, admittedly—I was in the clear. It would have been bad manners, if not bad ethics, to lie about my plants; but I wasn't lying, I was merely being a good salesman.

It took two weeks to get a nibble. Meanwhile, on my first VeggieTrader foray, I paid twelve dollars for two shiso plants from a woman named Mira who lived a block away from me (shiso is a member of the mint family whose flavor brings to mind an older lamb lumbering through a field of cilantro).

Two aspects of the VeggieTrader experience became clear during Mira's and my eight e-mail messages, and subsequent 140-second-long in-the-flesh encounter. First, my meetings with fellow VeggieTraders would always be deeply charged affairs, shot through with an errant intimacy. (A total stranger? Is in my apartment? Stroking my foliage and nattering on about chlorophyll?)

Gradually, a kind of protocol regarding these errantly intimate meetings emerged. It was okay to bring or receive plants in containers of intense decrepitude, unless a higher quality of container had been promised. It was okay to ask to take fewer but not more plants than you'd agreed to. It was okay to leave a swapper's residence the moment the plant reached your hands, without asking any personal questions or having complimented their breakfast nook. But it was not okay to have practiced false advertising, or to expect that your swapee would adopt any of the nicknames or gender assignments that you had foisted on the plant.

The second thing I realized was that the VeggieTrading vibe proved to be the opposite of cutthroat: Once the initial fizz of Mira's and my realization that we were both attractive, young, creative New Yorkers who liked esoteric soapy-mutton-tasting flora had dissipated, I had to persuade her to let me pay for her plants. She wanted to give them to me. And it felt oddly like trying to purchase, rather than legitimately adopt, a third-world-born infant.

I fell in love with my next trader—a tiny hipster in her twenties named Rebecca—before I'd even met her, and not just because she was the first person to respond to my ads. Her many voluble e-mails were flattering: "Your pepper plant sounds beguiling," she wrote of young Béla. Not to mention excitable: when I expressed interest in her cilantro seeds and Swiss chard seeds but not some of her other offerings, she wrote, "What?! No tomato? NO STRAWBERRY PLANTS? Dude, I'm begging you here! Get me out from under this jungle!"

When we met at the Union Square Greenmarket to swap, we each brought the other a special treat. Rebecca graced me with twenty-five—yes, that's twenty-five—strawberry seedlings, wrapped in damp paper towels, about the size of two fists. I brought her a potted fourteen-inch-and-growing vine that would produce woman melon (this being a fragrant yellow-fleshed fruit the size of a honeydew melon).

Rebecca whooped: "Wow! Woman melon!" She said she had looked it up on the Internet and had found only photographs that were not safe for work. I confessed that I was swapping the woman melon because "she needs more goddess energy than I can give her." Rebecca handed me two extra plastic bags she'd brought along, in case I needed them.

I planted Rebecca's bounty in fourteen terra-cotta pots; my apartment looked as if it had majored in liberal arts at Reed. Fired up by the rampant generosity I had encountered in my three VeggieTraders, I decided to take a new tack in my brokering: I would now simply give plants away. No money, no swapping—pure gift. I'd come to the decision that I should share my bounty because I had all I needed: My strawberry crop threatened to be the biggest thing in fruit since Violet Beauregarde. Moreover, I'd decided, somewhat grandiosely, that my plants were metaphors—mere symbols of the real growth taking place somewhere far more meaningful: deep within my man melons.

But then I had a flash of liberal guilt: If I'm giving my plants away, is that an unfair trade practice within the tiny economy that is VeggieTrader? Though none of the other New York City residents I'd swapped with were subsistence farmers, I decided that the truly thoughtful person would, prior to placing an ad saying he was giving away a basil plant, check to see if there was already an ad placed by someone else trying to sell a basil plant. And then stall if so.

Which I did. Nevertheless, I soon found myself standing on the edge of a large metropolitan park, holding a bag full of herbs to give to a man in his late forties with a shambling gait—never has the word *traffic* seemed more apt for my activities. A few days after that, a shy, young belly-dance instructor came to my office and hauled off three plants in a shopping cart.

I was spreading my proverbial seed far and wide. But was I being botanically promiscuous? In an effort, as the politicians say, to "reenergize my base," I decided to get in touch with Mira and Sander and Rebecca. Hoping I wasn't being overly forward or stalker-y, I sent each of them a recent photo of their plants, to show them the loving environment I'd been trying to provide their offspring. Was this too much? I spent an evening thinking that Mira might be creeped out by my e-mail.

But then, forty-eight hours later, having predicted that only Rebecca would write me back, I was tickled when all three of my fellow VeggieTraders did. Each congratulated me. Rebecca reported that the Woman and Béla were now regnant over a backyard in Queens; I promised Sander some of my first pumpkins, so he could make soup.

The world seemed tiny, friendly, glistening.

I flew out of JFK the other day, and as my plane soared over the huge galumphing sprawl that is Queens, I thought I detected a greenish bulge on the horizon.

Woman melon, was that you?

# VIII

*In which the author examines that group of people who—outside of dance instructors—are the most likely to swat at our collective ankles with their metal-tipped canes.*

This correspondent's quest to pin good manners to gelatin in the manner of a lepidopterist continued apace; never let it be said that the complications of protocol slowed me. Having now gone to Japan, and heard a lot of rude questions, and thought too much about Facebook, and lunched with Tim Gunn, I decided to round out my fieldwork by visiting the two entities most responsible for teaching manners in modern life: parents, and the manners mavens who sit on high and write the columns.

I have the utmost admiration for parents. Their task makes Emily Post's or Miss Manners's look like cheesecake. After all, everyone—or, let's estimate conservatively, 90 percent of us—who reads a manners column or book is doing so electively; we're a sympathetic audience, drawn in by the headliner or the bill of fare. But children come to the manners show after having had a net dropped over their heads.

Before a parent can explain to his child the intricacies of how to behave, he must first get his child to understand that there *is* a way to behave. When I reached out to colleagues and friends to ask them about their parenting strategies, this theme was struck repeatedly. As the writer and radio host John Moe, whose kids are nine, seven, and two, told me, "To a kid, manners are completely counterintuitive. Their instinct is to get things however they can. From an evolutionary standpoint, we are descended from the members of our species who are most aggressive because those are the kids who survived. No one wanted to breed with the meek because they were starving. So kids haven't unlearned all that yet. They see a cookie and they want to grab it and run away and eat it so no one else can get that cookie. But then here come Mom and Dad teaching them that the *right* way to get the cookie is to *ask*. And the thing about asking is, the answer could be no. So how is that a better way to get a cookie?"

A parent's task is made no easier by the fact that most children are ineluctably drawn to topics and objects of a slightly repulsive nature. Vani Kane, a development officer at Stanford University whose sons Tejas and Chetan are six and three, put it like this: "What's wrong with potty mouth at the dinner table? So what if I pick my nose and eat my findings? Why should these things bother anyone else? Kids like their bodily functions. They like the bodily functions of others. They like talking about them and can't imagine why no one else does."

Yes, tykes are not only unsuspecting, but they are also often also inherently rebellious. So...what can a parent do? "Our approach is to try to frame the entire concept of manners as a way of being nice. A Golden Rule thing," Moe told me. "When we have manners around other people, it's our way of being nice to them, of showing them that we want to be friends. That seems to work a little bit. After that we just employ the standard litany of bribes and empty threats to take us the rest of the way."

For some child rearers, the luck of the genetic draw is a strong factor. Sarah Thyre, whose kids are nine and four, told me, "What works is: You get a kid who gets the drift early in life. That kind of kid sees that, yes, it's better not to hit people or maraud with a butter knife in restaurants. The other kind of kid enjoys threats and malice, but hopefully you can teach that kid the humorous approach to such horrid things. Some kids seem to know from a relatively young age that you, the parent, can't really do jackshit. It's like they've noticed you're trying your damnedest to keep them alive and thriving, what're you gonna do if they misbehave—*kill 'em*? Noooooooo."

Knowing how *not* to instill your kids with manners can be just as important as knowing how to. "I get really annoyed by the kind of parent I call a 'narrator,'" says Thyre. "This is the parent that is commenting on every thing his child does, sometimes using the pronoun *we* as they do it, and making mild projections of what will happen in the near future: 'That's right, Caleb, we put the glass down gently, Caleb, gently, very good, right, Caleb, gently means soft, like we touch Rufus at home, right? Are we going to touch your doggy Rufus when we get home, Caleb? *Caleb.* Put the glass down because it's very delicate, Caleb...' Oh, I just want to vomit when I hear that. And I'm sure it's because I've been that person at some point. *But I decided to change, Caleb. I changed.*"

Narrators belong in novels, not restaurants.


## Prevaricain't


One of the toughest battlegrounds for parents is lying. It's in childhood that our mendacity gets its head start. In their book *NurtureShock*, authors Po Bronson and Ashley Merryman point out that most of the classic methods for promoting truthfulness work only to make kids better liars: "In studies, scholars find that kids who live in threat of constant punishment don't lie less. Instead, they become better liars, at an earlier age—learning to get caught less often."

*NurtureShock* recounts some of the experiments done by Dr. Victoria Talwar, a professor at McGill University, including one in which she reads children *The Boy Who*

*Cried Wolf* (the version in which both the boy and the sheep are eaten because of his repeated lies) or *George Washington and the Cherry Tree* (in which Washington's father reacts, "George I'm glad you cut down that cherry tree after all. Hearing you tell the truth is better than if I had a thousand cherry trees"). Intriguingly, the kids who read the George Washington story proceed to lie less often in tests (boys by 75 percent and girls by 50 percent), while those read *The Boy Who Cried Wolf* proceeded to lie *more*.

Why? The boy who cried wolf pays the ultimate price. But kids already know that lies are punished (Bronson and Merryman point out that 38 percent of five-year-olds think profanity is a form of lying because they think lying is anything that gets you punished). But the George Washington story is inspiring to kids because George is the recipient of both immunity and praise for having told the truth.

According to Bronson and Merryman, if parents say to their kids "I will not be upset with you if you lied. It doesn't matter if you did," this won't curb lying, because it leads kids to think, My parents really wish I didn't do it in the first place, and if I say I didn't, that's the best possible option for making my parents happy. Nor does it work for parents to say "We won't be upset if you lie, and telling the truth will make you feel really good about yourself." What does is: "I will not be upset with you if you lied, and if you tell me the truth about it, I will really be happy."

Larry Merculieff, who has spent four decades in various political and managerial jobs serving his people, the Aleuts of the Pribilof Islands in Alaska, told me, "I stole twenty dollars from my grandfather when I was six. I wanted a plastic model from my village's canteen. So I bought it. But unbeknownst to me, my aunt was standing behind me in the canteen."

I said, "Ouch."

"Yeah. Twenty dollars was a lot of money at that time for my people—we were destitute and living on subsistence hunting and fishing. So my aunt said 'Good morning' to me, then nothing more till we left the store. Then, once outside, in a gentle, non-accusatory voice, she asked me, 'Larry, where did you get the money for that?' I said, 'I stole the money from Grandpa.' She said, 'What do you think you should do about that?' I said, 'I guess I should take the plane back and give the money back.' She just nodded her head. We went into the canteen, and I gave the plane back. Then she took some money out of her pocket and bought it for me. When I returned the money to my grandfather, he said, 'Good boy.'"

I asked, "And did any single part of you think, Maybe I should try to steal something *even better* next time, and maybe they'll buy me that, too?"

"No. I never stole again."

## What Maxi Can't See

But of everything I read about parenting or heard from parents, the thing that left the biggest impression on me was something called "theory of mind." This is the ability to ascribe points of view and feelings to others, and to understand that these points of view and feelings might be different from one's own. (It's like reverse alcoholism.) Typically, theory of mind kicks in around age four. Prior to that, children have difficulty discerning their own and others' "false beliefs"—beliefs that conflict with reality.

The classic theory of mind test is as follows: A boy named Maxi places some chocolate in a kitchen cabinet and goes off to play. His mother enters the kitchen and puts the candy in a drawer, without Maxi's seeing her do so. The child who is being tested is then asked, When Maxi returns, where will he look for the chocolate—in the cabinet or the drawer?

Studies show that children at thirty months respond to such false-belief questions correctly about one fifth of the time; kids at forty-four months, about half the time; and kids after forty-eight months, almost all the time. (Regardless of their age, children with autism will tend to think that Maxi will look in the drawer.)

The more I thought about Maxi and his chocolate, the more I realized that it was providing me with a new definition for manners. Don't focus on the fact that the mother is clearly a bit of a bitch. No. Think of the kid being tested. You might want to label the great leap forward that he makes as "empathy"—but I think there's a better word.

I'd previously thought of manners as a worldview in which you cleaned off a public toilet seat in order to dodge blame. Or I thought of them as a way to deal with having dropped a customer's apple on the ground before putting it in his grocery bag. Now I started to think differently. After all, both of those definitions of manners refer back to the self—the toilet seat wiper is dodging blame, the grocery store clerk is trying to do his job well.

But maybe good manners are more outward-directed in nature than I'd originally thought. Maybe good manners are your ability to take on another person's point of view *regardless of your own*. Maybe good manners require momentary but total bodily transference.

Maybe good manners are imagination.

Come with me now to a very crowded, pre-holiday Penn Station, where I'm anxiously waiting to take a train up to Hartford, Connecticut, to visit my brother. It's early Saturday afternoon; the station is a hive of bodily jostling and sinister fluorescent lighting. My eyes are riveted on the departures board: I'm determined, once the track is announced, to push my way through the crowd so that I can get a seat on the train.

I notice an unshaven man in his sixties, wearing

sneakers, a blue windbreaker, and a facial expression of high distractedness. He's walking up to people—he's walking up very close to people—and asking, "Help the homeless?," to little effect. There's a lot of cold shoulder in the room. Everyone else is concentrating on the departures board, too.

But just then something clicks in my head—a perverse impulse to help others?—and when the man gets within eight or so feet of me, I walk over and hand him some loose change.

I tell him, "You know, you might do better if you stand in one place, and let people approach *you* rather than you walking up to *them*. It's less jarring."

"I was standing over there…"

He points toward the bathrooms.

"Well, there are cops over there," I say. "Cops make a lot of people feel guilty, so that probably wasn't in your favor."

I look off to the left and suggest, "What about over by that column?"

I point to one of ten huge metal columns holding up the ceiling, all lined up in two corridors along the side of the station's main waiting room.

The man drifts away, and I lose sight of him.

But about five minutes later, as I exit the bathroom and scurry back to a good position beneath the departures board, I see him standing in front of the column I'd pointed at.

When he sees me, I lift my eyebrows and tilt my head in the gesture that is universally recognized as *So?*

He lifts up his right arm, in whose hand he is clutching a one-dollar bill such that his index finger is pointing at the bill's presidential portrait.

He says, semi-triumphantly, "George."

# IX

*In which the author answers your mail.*

It came over me suddenly, without any exertion of will. It was a free-floating virus, and I was its human host.

Having steeped myself in manners lore both domestic and international, having formed the opinion that reverse apologizing is usually as rude as, if not ruder than, the incident that inspires it, I now sought an outlet for my burgeoning edification and long-standing opprobrium. Something that might transform my puny, flapping wind sock into a full-blown spinnaker.

And so I took to reading the letters written to etiquette columns, and then writing down, but not sending to anyone, my answers.

I'm particularly drawn to the etiquette column

in the English weekly *The Spectator*. One of its readers wrote in:

> I am shortly to attend a wedding. My problem is that I feel uneasy about kissing the bride as she stands in the receiving line because I am very aware of the dozens, if not hundreds, of lips that will have distributed various germs on to the same area of cheek I will be kissing myself. Would it be in order to make a little joke of my neurosis, bring out a facial cleaning wipe and dab her cheek with it before planting my kiss? Might she, indeed, be grateful to me for stripping off some of these accumulated DNA samples?

To which I "responded":

> This may not be the way to go here; indeed, it's possible that the only more inappropriate response would be a French kiss and an ass grope. And while it is true that some TV anchormen and former presidents are famous for carrying bottles of Purell with them to remedy all the germ-collecting they do while shaking hands with the hoi polloi, I assume that these gents are practicing their biocontainment on the sly.
>
> Your situation is why the air kiss and its handmaiden—the sound *Mwah!*—were invented. Make sure your eyes are full of sparkly deviltry as

you lavish these two items onto the space just next to the side, or sides, of their recipient's face.

Additionally, you might want to work on your pre-kiss exclamations. Few people ever remember the specifics of a social kiss unless it lands on their ear; but some will remember the "Congratulations!" or the "Your new _____ is *ravissant*! A poem!" Not to mention the varying levels of genuineness and creativity with which they are proffered. A genuine exclamation + an air kiss = warmth. A forced or disingenuous exclamation + an air kiss = a warning sign.

Wrote another *Spectator* reader:

I was invited to a very informal kitchen supper by a friendly neighbour and his wife. It would be just the three of us, and I strolled round there in anticipation of an enjoyable few hours of exchanging indiscretions. My problem is that when I walked into the kitchen I saw an open laptop—at one end of the table laid for three—in the fourth place as it were. The screen showed a man I had not met before waving, apparently at me, and raising a glass of wine in my direction. My host boasted that he had just got Skype which would enable us to "have dinner" with this man, another great friend of his, who lives in Johannesburg but who could see us in a camera in the laptop at our end. I must admit I was disappointed by this virtual intrusion. Conversation was buoyant but somehow artificial and we could not gossip. My friend soon tired of the novelty and began making faces at me but we could think of no way of politely disconnecting the friend in South Africa.

I had this to say:

A virtual guest! You are modern!

Given that you and your host were in agreement as to the fourth party's non-desirability, you might have colluded. It shouldn't have been difficult to think of a reason why the transmission of the laptop should suddenly go haywire: Computer malfunctions are God's way of keeping us humble. A sudden switching off of the router, followed by a frantic and apologetic phone call or PDA-originated e-mail, would have done the trick. An asteroid hit the house.

Had you and your host *not* been in agreement, then you would have had simply to grin and bear it. Which, given the scenario's juiciness as an anecdote to be told later, seems a small price to pay.

How was the veal?

Finally:

I have a dear friend, a dear bumbling fool of the old school who occasionally is driven to use the services of a prostitute. In the past he has always found them by looking out for immodestly dressed women who are standing in the street smoking with one foot against a wall. Now that so many of these women are, in fact, lawyers who are just having a smoking break outside their office, I am concerned that he might get into serious trouble. How should I advise him?

My thoughts:

Delicately.

～ﾟﾟ～

When I first started "writing" my various columns, I tried not to determine how *I* would answer these letters, but how the manners maven would. But I soon found that this effort at literary ventriloquism was missing that little something extra.

To me, it turned out, the joy was in responding to "my" readers' problems myself, with absolutely no accountability whatsoever. When you don't have to worry about precisely what Desperate in Dallas is going to do with your suggestion that he stop parking his car in the handicapped spot just outside his town's liquor store, you can instead focus on more writerly concerns like developing your worldview and voice. Which, for a beginner in the manners-dispensing arts like me, is more valuable.

There's no training or pedigree required of manners mavens—Letitia Baldrige, having served as Jacqueline Kennedy's chief of staff, is one of the few ones, if not the only major one, to have feet-on-the-ground experience in the field. But that doesn't mean you get out of bed one day and start cracking your ebony-handled whip. No, learning to give advice tactfully, I was finding, is a tightrope act. On the one hand, you want to be omniscient, gentle, loving, sensitive, practical, subtle, clear, objective, and kind; on the other, you don't want to be the most boring person on the planet. A voice of concerned objectivity that sounds like A Voice of Concerned Objectivity won't have its desired effect. It's like room tone played at deafening volume.

The five columns I read with the most avidity are Mary Killen's wonderfully witty one in *The Spectator*; an online one for the transgendered, called Miss Laura's TransTerrific Advice Column; Miss Manners; Philip Galanes's Social Q's in *The New York Times*; and Dan Savage's sexual advisory, Savage Love.

When devising your response to etiquette columns, it's naturally much more fun to disagree with the manners maven; you learn more this way, since you're forced to solidify or retinker your opinion. When a reader wrote in to Miss Laura's TransTerrific Advice Column to say he was transitioning from male to female—and wondered how best to tell friends and family—Miss Laura focused almost entirely on the writer. I, by contrast, focused almost entirely on the friends and family. Laura thinks it's important to prepare for the worst by making friends with other people who are also transitioning, in case your friends and family are unsupportive to your change of life. She advocates sending your friends and family letters that are accompanied by research found on the Internet.

My approach differed:

There are two ways for you to go here: town hall, or tête-à-tête. The former approach—like breaking up with someone in a restaurant—may have the advantage of putting a lid on the emotions of those who are rattled by the news. The latter has the advantage of precision: In talking to people individually or in small groups, you can tailor your commentary to their particular sensibilities. (It's imperative with this second approach, of course, that you swear your interlocutors to secrecy—Mother will be doubly disappointed if she finds out that she holds third spot on the phone tree.)

You probably want to explain your decision in a clear, unemotional manner that demonstrates how long and hard you have been thinking about this new direction for yourself. Express sympathy for, or at least understanding of, any social awkwardness you might be putting others in. Say that if any jerks or bigots connected to your friends or family need bullying, you are a new woman now, and thus able to embody the active verb *bitchslap*.

Though family members of heterosexuals would rarely ask that heterosexual about the details of his sex life, it happens often to people of alternative sexuality. I've heard many instances of gay men coming out to their families, only to be asked, How do gay men have sex? So unless your family is especially progressive, you should expect this. Expect a certain preoccupation with what's going on with you "down there." (Maybe, regardless of whether you've chosen a town hall or a tête-à-tête approach, you might be prepared with both a generalized, blanket summation of "down there," and then a later, more clinical chalk talk for those who crave hard data.)

Throughout, try to be indulgent of others' squirreliness. Even though you know that a change of gender doesn't mean a change of personality, they may not.

Much of the time that I "answer mail," though—particularly in the cases of Miss Manners and Philip Galanes in the *Times*—I agree with the maven's prescriptions, but differ on phrasing.

When one Miss Manners reader wrote that his atheism

was the source of social unease, and wondered how to react when people made churchy statements about others like "She's in a better place now," both Miss Manners and I agreed that such passing comments should be dealt with as if they were casual conversation. Moreover, we both agreed with the reader that the statement "I choose not to worship a deity" was a pompous statement for a non-believer to make. (Miss Manners also thought that such a statement was "challenging," and that you should simply say casually "I'm not a churchgoer"; I added that it was almost as grand as that bit of film noir dialogue that runs, "I don't go to church. Kneeling bags my nylons.") Overall, Miss Manners was far more succinct than I was, stressing that if the reader were to state his own religious convictions, he'd be doing exactly what he was reacting against, and therefore the best policy is to deflect without seeming to be giving in. I, on the other hand, thought you might downplay, aw-shucks, or apologize when put in this situation by breezily saying you "hate" or are "unable" to talk about faith, perhaps adding, if needed, "Faith is such a heavy, difficult thing to talk about. It really needs a mountaintop or a bottle of wine."

The net result of this comparing-and-contrasting is an increased appreciation for Miss Manners. She packs her prose with voice and personality, yet offers advice that is applicable to anyone.

Sometimes, a little egoism isn't a bad thing, however. Take Mary Killen of *The Spectator*, for example. The joy of reading her responses comes in seeing an eccentric vision tangle with the mundanities of life. Both she and her readers are regularly inventive and surprising. But she seems to take my guerrilla manners enforcement—in theory, at least—a good bit farther. Irritated by someone talking on his cell phone on the train? Record his conversation on your own cell phone, and then play back this recording at high volume. Sick of listening to your gym neighbor sing in the shower each morning? Have a third party berate you, not the offender, such that the offender can overhear the berating and be suffused with ambient humiliation. Fed up with your friend—we all know her, it's probably the same person worldwide—who calls you regularly to monologize but never asks anything about you? Withhold all information about your personal life for a period of time, and then have a friend ask the monologizer about one of your actual life dramas; and when the monologizer says she had no idea that you had such an obstacle in your life, have the friend say "But you talk to her every day for an hour!"

Indeed, Killen loves to remedy problems via the insertion of a third party, actual or metaphorical. A letter from one of her readers:

The new fashion of wearing pants that do not fit properly and reveal their underwear is in full flight here. There's no hope for the young, who will slavishly follow whatever is in fashion, regardless of how stupid it looks. However we have a friend in her late thirties or early forties. She is still quite an attractive woman for her age, but not so attractive that she should be wearing these sorts of things. What can we say to her, without appearing to be perverts or fuddy-duddies, to stop her wearing her pants so that her g-string underpants and the top part of her buttocks are showing to all and sundry?

Killen's response opens with the delightful reflection, "One school of thought holds that people's sartorial lapses should be welcomed, not suppressed. In an age where cosmetic surgery is impeding full communication, they offer vital non-verbal clues to compatibility." She then goes on to suggest a most unusual way of conveying the unflattering nature of the on-display underwear.

Do this by soliciting an opinion—which you can be confident will be approving—from an elderly and unattractive satyr in your network.

Let's call the satyr Les Patterson. Then you can tell your friend honestly, "By the way, you've got a fan in Les Patterson. He always defends you."

"What do you mean he always defends me?" she will naturally respond. "Defends me over what?"

"Oh, you know," you can smile pleasantly, "when fuddy-duddies and perverts are saying you shouldn't be wearing thongs and having your buttocks on show at your age. Les always says he thinks you look really raunchy and up for it."

Shoot, score!

I, meanwhile, thought the way to go here was to try to get your friend to joke about the way that hip-hop kids and inner-city youth are often displaying plumber's crack, perhaps offering the statement "I always want to put a pencil in there." I added that I didn't think you would need to be explicit about the parallel between her and the *hip-hopoisie*, "Just dangle it in front of her like a fetid carrot."

## The Home Version

I've tried various times to figure out why I am drawn to etiquette columns, but it's hard work. I'm not sure I can parse it.

I remember reading an interview from *Der Spiegel* with the Italian author Umberto Eco, who had just curated a show at the Louvre about lists, in conjunction with a book he'd written about the same topic.

Asked "Why lists?" Eco first proved evasive, offering, "I can't really say. I like lists for the same reason other people like football or pedophilia. People have their preferences."

But then, pressed further, Eco said, "We have a limit,

a very discouraging, humiliating limit: death. That's why we like all the things that we assume have no limits and, therefore, no end. It's a way of escaping thoughts about death. We like lists because we don't want to die."

What struck me about this statement is that it's so different from why I'm drawn to manners columns.

Sometimes, at the end of a busy day, I like to bury myself in a police procedural. Be it *Law and Order* or a paperback mystery that I bought for fifty cents in some unventilated church basement, a step-by-step solving of a crime is, to my addled brain, reassuring and calming. Only having a small child or pet fall asleep on top of me is more mooring.

Manners columns have a similar appeal. They reassure me and console me by suggesting that life's ragged edges can be made smooth, that there's never not an answer to even the most challenging question. They're finite, and devoid of the hundreds of extenuating circumstances that make the solving of my own or my friends' problems so complicated.

I'm not entirely certain that in a real-life situation, raunchy Les Patterson would provide anyone succor, or serve anyone given to showing her knickers as a useful cautionary tale.

But I like to believe that he would, because to do so is to make life seem manageable.

## X

*In which the author himself tries to wield a
metal-tipped cane, albeit one that is
visible only online.*

And yet, happy though I am to have the satyr Les
Patterson—or the idea of him—to provide sustenance in
my life, another part of me thinks that he's a crutch.

It's all well and good for someone like me, a dewy
beginner in the world of advice dispensing, to go around
saying that manners columnists have it easy, and that
manners columns are a kind of soothing palliative. It's
harder to put yourself into the line of fire, and actually
*dispense* advice to people in states of quandary.

And so I decided to talk my talk.

I went onto Facebook and told my friends that I was
willing to be their online etiquette coach. I asked them
to send me a description of their problems. Not wanting
to become a permanent sob sister, I stipulated that I was

offering my services for only six to eight weeks; thus, their problems should be ones that might be helped or even solved within this time period.

Eight viable responses came in. I warmly rejected the first one: A friend wrote that his mother had just been diagnosed with cancer and that his stepfather, with whom my friend was estranged, wanted to patch things up with my friend before the mother's demise. Oh, also: The stepfather wanted all the patching-up to be done exclusively online.

The darkness of this scenario—as my friend had suspected—felt too large for my tiny penlight to illuminate. I begged off. My friend was wholly understanding; I told him to "go with God, or some other suitably large life force."

A friend who is a filmmaker and academic wrote to lament the way that her hipster friends—some, quiet literary men; some, academics; some, ebullient lesbian filmmakers—love to engage in poo-talk. (Having gotten the nod from groovy franchises like *South Park* and David Sedaris, frank discussions of feces and its transport are, to some, a sign of comedic enlightenment.)

Though I was excited about the prospect of investigating this topic, I worried that my friend might not encounter enough instances of poo-talk in the allotted time period. In the meantime, I encouraged her, when she found herself in the middle of fulsome conversations, either to feign boredom or to claim that her cell phone had vibrated so that she could then go "answer" it.

The third scenario that didn't "take" was that of a gentleman in Texas who wrote that after having a drink or two, he was prone to making ribald comments "about women other than my wife"; his wife either hears these comments or hears about them "in a 'your husband is a pig' sort of fashion."

To this blurter I wrote:

There's a writing exercise in which you write the same letter or note to three different people—your best friend, your boss, your ten-year-old son. All the information comes out the same in each, but the tone and references are slightly different in each.

Some of us in long-term relationships have difficulty remembering our audiences or who we're "playing to" because, at a certain point in the proceedings, the warmth we carry for our beloved starts to look and feel a lot like the warmth we carry for our dog or couch.

So, next time you throw one back, I suggest you try a variation on the writing exercise described above.

Don't even think of her as your wife. Think of her as a potential investor in your next start-up.

The Blurter and I fell out of touch over the next two months. I will confess that my prejudice toward this particular problem—chauvinism—when combined with my suspicion that the problem was unlikely to be reined in over the course of six or eight weeks, made me somewhat passive toward this "client." I did not badger him with e-mails, as I would some of my subsequent charges. My last communication from him was a group e-mail, sent to about fifty people, informing me that he had invented a new snack food. On reading this promotional plug, I scowled and thought, Facebook!

## The Five

Though it is probably unwise to look at my five full-on clients in terms of my success or nonsuccess with them, I cannot help but do so; I am human and prone to quantifying.

And so I report that I had two successes, one semi-success, one uncertainty, and one miss.

I had my best results with Tom O'Leary, a filmmaker in Los Angeles. On one of that city's more glittering dance floors, Tom had met a fetching gentleman we'll call Jesse. After dancing together, Jesse went home with Tom. When, in the wee hours, Jesse was getting ready to leave Tom's place, Tom suggested they exchange phone numbers; Jesse hesitated and gave Tom his e-mail address instead.

"The next day," Tom wrote me, "being the 13-year-old girl that I am, I looked Jesse up on Facebook. What I discovered is that he works for an old New York friend of mine at a restaurant here in LA. So I sent Jesse an e-mail that read 'Last night was awesomely fun. Let me know when you would like to do something again sometime. Just saw your profile on Facebook. Guess what? [Your boss, the chef] is an old friend of mine from New York. I won't mention to him our night last night. Thanks again. Loved making you shiver. Tom.'"

Tom received no response from Jesse, so a week later wrote again.

Jesse wrote back, "Hi, Sorry but I'm kind of a one-time fling kinda guy and have to keep things in the closet and very private from friends and family. Hope you understand. Have a great time in Palm Springs. ;-) take care."

Tom asked me, "So, etiquette-wise, how do I respond? Wish him luck in his closeted life?"

The correct tack here, I imagine, would be, Don't respond. On the met-in-a-club front: These things never last. On the he's-closeted front: These things never last.

Yet I had a strong sense that Tom was not a quitter.

In the interest of not repelling Tom, I decided not to chastise him for the indiscretion about Jesse's boss. I wrote him:

We are not wholly ourselves when we date. I always cut people a lot of slack for their behavior during any of my first three dates with them—largely because I know how braggy, neurotic, and needy *I* am under the spotlight.

But this guy's letter is of another order.

The only way to go wrong here is to write an angry letter. No response at all is how most of us would choose to operate, regardless of whether we're still interested in this closeted gent or not. (If we're still interested: nothing says you reciprocate his disinterest quite like resounding silence. If we are still interested: we're playing hard to get.)

If you feel betrayed by him (because you didn't know he was closeted) and you feel a need to tell him this, don't write this e-mail when you're angry. Moreover, once you've written it, wait 24 hours and re-read it. On the basis of one date, you haven't built up enough equity really to launch into him. And yet…sure, if—on behalf of all men this guy will go on dates with in the future—you want to write a note saying you wish you'd known this crucial fact about your friend, you're wholly entitled.

If you *are* still interested in pursuing a relationship with him, beware. Don't get hurt.

And if you're interested in pursuing this guy purely for the sex: enjoy. But expect lots of sudden delays.

When Tom wrote me back, he acknowledged his indiscretion about Jesse's boss:

I understand, and you've probably intuited, that I believe I scared Jesse off (even more than he would have normally been scared off) when I mentioned that I knew his boss. If Jesse is as closeted as he seems to be I probably sent him into a panic with my original e-mail.

The complication is that I've never been to my friend's restaurant and my friend is annoyed with me about that, so I am finally going to have dinner there this coming Thursday. If Jesse is there he will probably think I am stalking him.

At this point in the scenario I had to make the crucial distinction between being a life coach and an etiquette coach. The former would here scream, "Tom, honey! You're kidding yourself if you think you're going to that restaurant to sample your chef friend's osso buco! Do not turn the light on in that closet!" Then I would wag my index finger snap diva-ishly in the air while exhorting, "Shut it down!"

But an etiquette coach, it struck me, has the less presumptuous task of trying to change not Tom, but rather his behavior.

I wrote:

The ideal manners here would be for you to peek in the windows of the restaurant before entering and, if you see Jesse, to wait to go to the restaurant on a night when he isn't working. Or, alternatively, to e-mail him in advance to say you're coming so that, if he's frantic about possibility of seeing you, he can try to switch shifts with someone else.

But these methods are fairly impractical, I realize—and I assume you're going to the restaurant primarily because you're hoping to see him. If you go and indeed he *is* working, you probably want to be as discreet as possible—a small nod of the head is probably as much effusiveness as you want to offer. Anything more is likely to make him uncomfortable—as would your trying to ignore him in the restaurant altogether, which might seem stalker-y.

If it turns out that not only is he working, but is, in fact,*your waiter*, then, obviously, that calls for something different: in this case I think you should address the awkwardness in some lightly comedic way, just to try to dispel it.

When I hadn't heard from Tom by about two PM on the day after the intended restaurant visit, I sent a noodgey e-mail asking him how it went and if he had e-mailed before going. He wrote back:

So I followed your advice and did give Jesse a heads-up. I got this response: 'thank you for the heads up. i hope you understand that I won't be able to talk as I would not be able to explain how we met and it would jeopardize my friendships and future at work and make it very uncomfortable to continue working here.' So I sent this quick response: 'Got it. No problem. I will act as if we never met. Be well. I wish u the best.'

I got to the restaurant with my friend Holly. The place was huge, chaotic and busy. A young woman greeted us. Just then Jesse came around a corner and saw me and winced and immediately looked away. Jesse was asked to show a big party to their table and left with the party. Another person showed us to our table. I never saw Jesse again for the entire night.

I think, in retrospect, that when I sent the first e-mail to Jesse I should never have mentioned that I knew the Executive Chef at his restaurant. It never occurred to me that Jesse might be in the closet and have a life that is compartmentalized.

Because he seems so paranoid about anyone finding out about this marginalized part of his life I will not contact him again.


Tiny victory! I experienced a feeling of completion and satisfaction; my veins coursed with puppetmastery.

But two days later, something occurred to me. I wrote Tom, "By continuing the narrative with Jesse, as you did, you probably needed to be willing to deal with, and/or help him with, his coming out. Did that occur to you? Would you have been willing?" Tom answered:

> The answer is a definite Yes! I would have been willing to do almost anything to stay "connected" with Jesse. When I got up in the middle of dinner to use the restroom, I was fantasizing (thanks to the wine) that I would run into Jesse in the cavernous bathroom and he would pull me into a stall and we would have a Lady Gaga video moment and ravish each other. What I hope I haven't done is push Jesse further back into the closet.

Moreover, Tom had a new question. His friend, the chef, "made me promise to come back and dine very soon. Should I warn Jesse every time I go to the restaurant?"

Once again, my inner life coach started screaming. "Tommy! Shut. It. Down!"

But instead I listened to the cool breezes of the etiquette gods. I told Tom no—he had now proven his ability to be discreet in Jesse's presence. Further contact would only heighten Jesse's anxiety. Less is more—or less, or nothing.

I refrained from telling Tom to start patronizing one of Los Angeles's other thirty-five thousand restaurants.

## Hell Is Other People

Getting Tom to warn Jesse of his imminent arrival at Jesse's restaurant was pretty thrilling for me. The e-mail warning was the kind of gesture that, had I been in that situation myself, I would fully intend to do, but wouldn't actually get around to—the kind of thing I'd do only if I knew someone was watching.

My other success was in conjunction with an equally peculiar scenario. My friend Matthew, a sales manager at a medium-size exporter-importer in Seattle, sent it in. A colleague whom Matthew is friendly with at work, but doesn't hang with outside the office, returned from maternity leave one day. Matthew ran up to her to give her a hug and to congratulate her on the miracle of birth. At which point the woman—let's call her April—said to him, "So you'll give me a hug now but you won't text me congratulations when the baby was born?" Then she turned and walked away.

As had Matthew and his wife, I chalked the woman's response up to hormones. I added:

> People who are celebrating peak moments in their life have no right to dictate how we acknowledge these moments (unless we do so in an offensive manner, which you haven't); this new mother's insistence on a text message would be no better if she'd specified, "I

was hoping you'd send a Far Side greeting card with a drawing of turkey vultures."

I'd suggest you proceed as if she hadn't made the strange request. Ask about the baby, ask about Mom's health—but as before. If she continues to be weird, simply say—as is probably the case—"Hey, I didn't want to barrage you with yet-another-text that you'd feel like you had to answer at a very busy and emotionally fraught moment in your life."

If she still seems hurt, then tell her you'd like to talk about the situation. Do so. If you're moved to say "I'm sorry," you should apologize for the misunderstanding, not for what you did (or didn't do).

April had just started working part-time, so Matthew didn't run into her during the next month. However, he wrote me twice during that time, once to tell me:

I absolutely agree with your advice not to initiate a discussion about it. If there is obvious tension about it that just won't quit, I'll use the "seek to understand, then be understood" principle, asking her, "what was it that most bothered you about not seeing a text from me?" and reassuring her that I only want the best for her and her daughter and I am happy for her, but I just didn't feel our relationship was on a level where a congratulations from me was expected. I can then say that I sometimes forget to call my close relatives for their birthdays and other events when my acknowledgment is expected. This guy is just not the Hallmark card type.

Like you said, though, the one thing I will not do is apologize, even for the misunderstanding. Since no fault is felt from this side of the table. I'm telling you—"I'm Not the Hallmark Type" is a great song title.

I wrote Matthew, "Sounds good." I added, "The beauty of 'I'm Not the Hallmark Type' is that it could be either an angry rock anthem, or a heartfelt country ballad. You could go either Iggy or Merle."

Ten days later, lightning struck:

Soooooooo. [April] came back to the office Monday. We had a meeting together on Monday with a few other people and we both ignored the issue.

Then today I passed by her when she was alone in her office. She asked if she could talk to me about something personal. I shut the door. She brought up the comment she made and said she was surprised that so many people from work, including the VP, e-mailed or gave her some good wishes, with the exception of her peers, which included me. She said it hurt her because we worked so closely together.

I told her that my intention was only wanting the best for her and her baby, and that I'm very happy for her. However, I didn't feel like we had that personal a relationship and didn't want to encroach on her during what was a difficult and busy time. Plus, I told her, I'm horrible at remembering events even for close members of my family. She was cool with that; the tension dissolved and the conversation drifted off onto other topics for about a half hour. She ended it by saying, "It was important for me to tell you that." I replied, "My intention was sound, but I'm just a clueless dude. Thanks for telling me how you feel."

I had my semi-success with Lapata, a painter in New Hampshire who has an infant daughter. Lapata had asked me, "How does one approach other moms in settings such as the playground, the grocery store, etc. and arrange play dates? It always makes me feel like I am hitting on people if I broach this subject out of the blue, and some women actually act like they are being pursued too aggressively."

I wrote:

I feel your pain. Whenever I chat up people who are standing alone at a party, I am always made to feel like I've scrawled my hotel room number on their inner thigh with a lipstick.

Three possible approaches suggest themselves. The first is to seize the truth of your situation, and simply to state it semi-comically to your new acquaintances: "I always feel like I'm hitting on other moms when I ask them for a playdate," or, "I would ask you for a playdate but every time I've tried doing it, people act like I've rubbed my body up against theirs," etc. This might defuse the awkwardness. It will at the very least generate conversation. (Also: you probably don't want to ask a lot of personal questions, particularly at first.)

Another route available to you is somehow to pique these other parents' interest so that they actually HOPE you'll ask for a playdate, or so that they ask YOU for one. An innocent but slightly mysterious remark, uttered casually, can do much to intrigue the uninitiated ear—maybe something along the lines of: "My daughter and I are spilling a lot of cider these days in the hope of turning our home into a human glue trap." Or, maybe something like, "According to my daughter, there are tiny people living inside my salt shaker."

The third route is perhaps the least savory but possibly the most effective and time-honored. It is simply to brag about, or vaunt, playdates with OTHER children that you and your daughter have had. Everyone wants to be on a winning team.

Lapata wrote back a few hours later to thank me; she explained that her plan would probably be sprung into action at the weekly farmer's market, which she described as "THE social event in town": a place where "all the babies and baby mamas assemble on little quilts on a patch of green next to the performer, usually a folksy fiddler."

Two days later, knowing that a farmer's market had come and gone, I wrote Lapata to ask if she'd engineered any "hot playdate action." She wrote back an hour later to report that she'd made no headway, but added, "I am going to keep on trying, though!" Sensing an eager pupil, I fired back, "Keep at it, Tiger!" Seconds later, I rued having called someone Tiger.

A week later, I checked in again. Lapata wrote:

So the next farmer's market, I went into the fray fully prepared to be brazen and forward. After surveying the crowd, I spied a mother of three children with whom I had spoken previously. One of her children is just a few months older than Serafina, and coincidentally, we had seriously considered buying their house (which she knew about). About a month ago, we had talked for five or ten minutes and it had been very friendly.

I saw this as a clear opportunity. I walked up to her confidently bearing my baby in my arms. She was also holding her baby, so it all seemed quite easy all of a sudden. When I got up close, I saw that she was chatting with a woman near her but it didn't look too intimate or serious. I stood right next to her and pointed out the other baby to Serafina, which I thought of as the proper approach. She did not look at me and continued her conversation with the other woman, which seemed to be about logistics for some child party: parking, swimming, etc. I thought, Well, this will end momentarily, and then she will turn and speak to me. However, she did not. The logistics conversation continued for some time, during which I felt that she must notice me, and I was sure she could see me since I was standing right next to her and looking at her. Suddenly they stopped speaking and she turned to say something to one of her other children, fully facing me. Then she walked off across the green. Such rejection! I have been unable to crawl out of my shell since, though I shall try again this Thursday, I promise.

I responded:

Oh, so close! Foiled by a Chatty Cathy!

As with dating, it's the approaching the other person that's the most terrifying part. If you and S. were to sit on your blanket with an especially alluring toy, maybe you would draw others—initially, children—to you?

I didn't hear from Lapata for two weeks. Fearful that I was approaching Noodge status, I did nothing.

But then a week later I couldn't help myself: I checked in.

Lapata wrote back:

So after two weeks of feeling like a loser on the dance floor, I went back to the farmers market with renewed energy, but also a bit of the nonchalance one feels when there's nothing left to lose. This happened to coincide, it turned out, with Serafina suddenly beginning to interact with other children. We sat down in the area populated mostly by parents and small children, and she rushed off and sat near the musicians. She was wearing her very attractive purple sunglasses. A little girl who is older than her by about six months followed her over there, entranced by the sunglasses. They sat and interacted minimally for a while. The other little girl's parents were sitting next to me, so this forced them to interact with me. Both the little girls then came back and Serafina acted quite familiarly with them, eating some of their cheddar bread and even climbing into the lap of the mom. I tried awkwardly to make conversation with them, and they were only a tiny bit standoffish. Finally, when we were leaving, I screwed up my courage and asked if they had a card with them and would they like to organize a play-date. They seemed a little surprised, but they were

amenable. I didn't bring up my feelings of awkwardness, but I must admit that having an etiquette coach
was what helped spur me on and go in for the kill.

I waited for a week and then wrote to the mother.
I also sent two photos I'd taken of the two little girls
playing. This seemed to charm her and she wrote
back right away with concrete dates for playing and
even invited us to her daughter's birthday party in
two weeks!

Ice cream, cake, tiny pools of purple vomit! A playdate is born.

By contrast, I couldn't tell if I helped P. J. or not. An
employee at an independent insurance firm in central Connecticut, she'd written to say that her office has cubicles
from wherein "my coworker bellows out requests, questions
and general information to us on a regular basis throughout
the workday. I ask her to shush and remind her that everyone can hear her. The bosses have asked her to lower her
voice, but everybody's too polite to *do* anything about it."

I offered five ideas in ascending order of direness:

DEFCON 1: A specific request is more effective
than a blanket one. Prior to making an important
phone call—be it actually important or just "important"—try telling your colleague about it. Then try
doing this two or three times during the next week,
but, instead of announcing your imminent phone

call to a client, simply point to your phone meaningfully.

DEFCON 2: I've twice lived on noisy streets and have had success placing a fan, operating at its highest speed, someplace where you can hear its whirr, but someplace that does not require you to glue all moveable objects to your desk.

DEFCON 3: If the problem persists, ask your boss to address it at a staff meeting. Making the problem a public one will inject it with a highly effective ingredient: humiliation.

DEFCON 4: If the problem persists: intervention.

DEFCON 5: Duct tape.

The response to my pedagogy started out well enough. One of P. J.'s blasts from the fray ran, in part:

I patiently listened to her story about the heatwave upsetting her dog's stomach which made the dog's poops soft and, when she came up for air, I told her I was planning to call a VIP client and would she mind keeping her voice low. My phone call was nearly completed when I heard her bawdy Laugh bellowing through the office. I loudly exclaimed, "Shh!" and she replied, "Oh, sorry."

Then P. J. walked over to the noisemaker's cubicle and pleaded with her. "She apologized and without taking a breath asked me how do I get any work done now that I'm right next to another co-worker who she thinks is loud."

Later, P. J. tried a fan, but said it didn't work.

Later still, the situation was discussed at a staff meeting, but that didn't help.

Some weeks later, the noisemaker was still noisemaking, yet the tenor of P. J.'s e-mails had grown resigned. Whether or not I had anything to do with this newfound resignation is unknown to me.

A month later, P. J. got a new job at a different company.

Intriguingly, my other non-success was also facing down a noisemaker. A friend I'll call Mei, who lives in Kansas, had waxed irritable about her friend, Jane, who kept trying to make Mei her "love-life coach."

Mei wrote, "On and on I hear about the crazy weekends and the hot sex. She's always asking me to weigh the hot sex vs. the fact that this Match.com date is a creationist or doesn't know who Andrew Jackson is. (I always pick the hot sex as stupid people are a dime a dozen.)" She added that hearing about all this carnality was making her "mad jealous."

I wrote:

I wish I could offer some subtle, sly subterfuge here—like encouraging you to draw your friend out on other topics, or having you tell her about a spiritual cleanse you are undergoing that requires total auditory purity.

But, alas, I think the only way to go here is to bite the bullet. You could start vague: "Hey, would you mind if we talk about something else?" If she doesn't go for this, then you can be more specific: ask if it'd be possible to talk about something other than her love life because you're starting to feel like the Joan Cusack/Rita Wilson/Elizabeth Perkins/Julie Kavner character in a chick flick. Your shoulder is damp.

If additional specificity is required, then you'll have to be blunter: "All this talk about your love life is starting to come between us." Whether or not you cop to your jealousy here is up to you and the nature of your friendship—I would encourage it, as it's honest and endearing; but I would also understand if you think it's too Pandora's boxy.

Mei wrote back:

You mean I actually have to follow this advice and not be a chickens***t and just complain about it? Oh.

Thinking I will take the humorous route, stealing your 80's–90's film references, and see how it goes. She's very Californian-New-Agey, that "auditory purity" line followed by a crazy hyena-like laugh could work, too.

Mei's story made me think about an interesting wrinkle in advice receiving: We tend to listen to those advice givers whose worldview is the most similar to our own. But often the truths we need to hear are the ones we least want to hear—and which don't necessarily come from people similar to us, who may be blind or resistant to the same modes of behavior that we are. So if we ally ourselves with one sole dispenser of wisdom, we may be cutting ourselves off from all sorts of potential epiphanies. Thus, maybe etiquette pantheism is the way to go; you increase your odds of hearing something that might make a difference.

As for Mei, three weeks later, the only sign of improvement was that, during a phone call, Mei had managed to change the subject successfully by asking, "When are we going to go for that cup of coffee?"

And then, minutes later, when Jane started in again, she added, "I promise I won't make it all about [the current object of her affections] when we meet."

I applauded Mei for her efforts, and encouraged her to keep drawing a line in the sand.

Over the course of the next month, however, Mei's e-mails described a dynamic that was unchanged: Jane kept nattering on about her inappropriate-but-hot men, and Mei kept listening and nodding.

My suspicion here was that Mei's friend was one of those people who are always asking for advice, but then never taking it. Some of these folks seem to do this simply so they can quietly debunk your counsel as they proceed with exactly the course of action that you tried to dissuade them from. Only now they're armed with counter-arguments to all possible objections.

These people: kind of irritating. "Despite all you said, I am still going to set this barn afire/buy that tangerine windbreaker/tell my sister-in-law what I really think about her porcelain wee Scottie figurines, and afterward you will wonder why I spent hours asking you what you thought I should do." When people do this repeatedly, what they're offering is not really an invitation for you to try to help them; what they're offering is a human Twitter feed.


## Retrospection

When I look back on my days as an online coach, I'm struck by the fact that it's easier to weigh in on scenarios where the manners adjustment needs to be made by a third party—but it's also harder to change them. For instance, it's fairly easy to tell someone how to deal with his obnoxious colleague or unsanitary neighbor; but it requires much more careful wording to advise someone who is himself obnoxious or unsanitary. Tom's and Matthew's and Lapata's cases, for instance, asked me carefully to encourage Tom and Matthew and Lapata to act in a certain way, which I did (and they did). But in the case of the two noisemakers, it was fairly effortless to think of plans of attack—which, ultimately, met with limited success. I chalk all this up to something I'll call "investment." The reason why I found success with Tom and Lapata and Matthew, but not with P. J.'s or Mei's talkers, seems fairly obvious: The former group was invested in their relationship with me in a way that the latter was not.

I was also interested to note that the success or non-success of each case had nothing to do with how well I knew these folks. When I'd first put my notice up on Facebook, I'd thought that increased intimacy would figure into things in either a good or a bad way—i.e., that knowing someone would make my insights more tailored and apt; or, conversely, that knowing someone well would have caused me to pull my punches out of politeness or deference.

But these concerns proved groundless. Rather, the sympathy I felt toward some of the projects was a factor: The chauvinism displayed by the Texan who blurts stuff out to his wife was inherently less endearing or interesting to me than, say, Tom's love travails or Lapata's need for playdates, and thus I pursued it less aggressively. You bring what you love into the house, where you give it a nice rinse in the kitchen sink; everything else stays out in the driveway.

I would encourage anyone who's a good listener and who's interested in etiquette to offer up her services to her friends as I did. Not only is it a chance to help out other friends, but it also encourages you to define your world-view and recognize your blind spots.

That said, I would also warn you to prepare for exhaustion. Therapists take off the month of August, but I'll need at least a year.

## ~~ぐ XI ~~

*In which the author builds up a kind of shrine around the word* lovely, *and then tries to* lovely *it up with a swarm of foreigners, some of them German.*

A few years ago, at a Saturday matinee performance of the Holocaust drama *Irena's Vow*, starring Tovah Feldshuh, one theatergoer who'd arrived after the show had started asked Feldshuh, up on the stage, to wait for him to reach his seat. He shouted out to her, "Can you please wait a second?" Feldshuh acceded to his request.

What intrigues me about this anecdote is its polarity. When we hear the word *manners*, the other words that we tend to associate with it are *restraint*, *self-control*, *discipline*.

But on hearing the word *manners*, I was now thinking *imagination*, and trying my hardest not to be a crybaby-Maxi whining about his goddamn chocolate.

In the Spectator's-Request-During-*Irena's-Vow* example, we see the two remote poles of imagination—on the one hand, an actress, whose very profession it is to conjure up a person who is not herself; and on the other, a theatergoer whose solipsism verges on autistic. The actress bends over backward to be more than polite—she's breathtakingly accommodating; the audience member is a bulldozer in a china shop. And yet her extreme gracious-ness, for all the rest of us, made his boorishness go away fast and painlessly.

The more I thought about manners—and answered letters to columns, and acted as an etiquette coach—the more I realized that there's an economy of good manners. At the bottom are those acts done purely for the sake of survival—you share a piece of bread with a fellow pris-oner because you know he'll return the favor; you take a colleague's work shift so she'll take yours the following week. In the middle of the economy are those acts you do to keep the world running smoothly, perhaps with, but not always because of, your hope that the world will show you the same courtesy—you hold a door open for a stranger; you cover your mouth when sneezing. At the top are those acts that are pure altruism—you leave a baby stroller you no longer need out on the sidewalk for any-one to claim; you tell a random stranger that hers is the most beautiful skin you've ever laid eyes on.

Throughout our lives, we bounce from one part of the spectrum to another, often during the course of a single day. Some of us spend weeks bottomed out at the survival end of the list, living a quid-pro-quo, eye-for-an-eye life full of sidelong glances and sharpened incisors. But the more we're willing to shed our primitive selves and operate from our imaginations rather than from our physical needs, the more easily we can get to the higher part of the spectrum.

It's surprising, and maybe a little disappointing, that so few manners mavens have made great marks as activists or pioneers. One of the few, P. M. Forni, a Johns Hopkins professor of Italian literature, established the Johns Hopkins Civility Project in 1997. In addition to creating a library of books about civility, he has inspired two counties in Maryland to wage a massive "Choose Civility" campaign involving refrigerator magnets and bumper stickers, and has helped businesses to give out awards for good manners. (Forni's aha moment occurred while teaching Dante's *Divine Comedy* one day. He realized that "I wanted my students to know everything that there is to know about Dante," he told the *Johns Hopkins Gazette* in 2007, "but even if they did and they went out to be unkind to a little old lady on a bus, I would think that I had failed as a teacher.")

The word *manners*, when used on its own as an exhortation—"Manners!"—reminds one of what *not* to do. And so, too, with manners in general: Most people think of them as being "what you shouldn't do." A smaller group thinks "what you *should* do." But what if we all started thinking of them as "what you *might also* do"?

There's nothing stopping us from thinking of certain acts of philanthropy or activism or altruism as acts of good manners. There's nothing keeping us from all becoming a little more elf-like. For instance, I'd love to hear a Doctors Without Borders medic, just as he's about to insert his scalpel into the chest wound of a soldier who's fighting for a country that's at war with the doctor's own country, cry, "Manners!" That'd send a message.

## The Lovely G's

So...what can we imagine? If we lift up our heads and look past the basic courtesies—far beyond the pro forma, and several miles farther on from the rote—there's a sunny patch of land that I like to call The Isle of Lovely Gestures. [Sounds of birds twittering as they tie silken bows around the neck of docile cows in a woozily pastoral setting.]

This is a place that drips with potential. And while it may seem simplistic to offer up a list of ways to bring more honey-drenched sunsets into our own and others' lives, we have to start somewhere.

That somewhere is here.

- If you are going to an event with a partner or friend, and that person has more at stake than you (professionally, socially, or psychodramatically), it might be a Lovely Gesture to reach out to that person and have her help select what you're going to wear.

- If you have recently been the subject of scandal or grave illness, you will bring a certain amount of relief to your friends and colleagues if, once your pain has started to thaw and you're ready to reengage with life, you check in with members of your circle on some matter unrelated to the scandal or illness. This sends a signal that normalcy has resumed, and that an interaction with you does not need to have the emotional tenor of a public radio segment on Darfur.

- If someone sends you a gift certificate, why not send that person a photo of what you bought? If someone sends you *any* gift, why not send them a photo either of The Gift in Action or The Gift at Rest?

- In Japan, people on escalators will stand flush right if they are merely riding on, but not walking up, that escalator. This gives wide berth to the time-constrained and the athletic.

- Should you need to return to its rightful owner a cell phone that you've found, it's best to be as discreet as possible. On finding that there's no information identifying the owner of the phone, you'll probably call the first, or most recently used, number in the phone's call history. Consider the possibility that the owner of the phone is having an affair—possibly *with* the person you have called, or possibly is *cheating on* the person you have called. Thus, it might behoove you not to reveal where exactly you found the phone. Or what if this cell phone owner called in sick that day, and you call his boss to say you've found his employee's cell phone at a basketball game?

• If two people are staying in a hotel room, it is highly hospitable if one or the other of them gets into the habit of sometimes using the bathroom located off the hotel's lobby, particularly for his lengthier sit-downs. To do so is to reduce aroma and anxiety, disperse foot traffic, and inject mystery into the relationship.

• Guests, particularly if they are to intermingle with people they don't know, are sometimes put at ease if you give them something to talk about. It might be as simple as saying to them, shortly after they've arrived, "You'll definitely want to view the new soap dispenser in the bathroom." Show them the sculptural cherubim onto whose face you've glued a photograph of your spouse. Or start a rumor that, an hour into the gathering, a yoga clown will arrive.

At the risk of name-dropping: I once went to a friend's house for a party held in honor of Elizabeth Gilbert, who had just returned from the trip that she would write up in *Eat, Pray, Love*. As you entered, Gilbert would pin onto your shirt a cloth certification patch of the kind you might earn at summer camp; I was "Small Craft Navigation." Once you have "Small Craft Navigation" pinned to you, it's almost impossible to experience awkwardness when talking to others. You'd be amazed by how much people have to say on the topic of rope.

- If you're at a small gathering at which the only person not drinking is someone who is newly on the wagon or is known to be having troubles staying on the wagon, then it might be thoughtful for you to refrain from drinking, too. You've been trying to cut back anyway.

- Talking to people with cancer or incurable diseases can make you second-guess yourself a lot. Poet Nikki Giovanni, who lost both her mother and sister to cancer in 1995 and later contracted the disease herself, said the best comments she received during her treatment were ones that presupposed her longevity. "I'm a music person, so friends would say 'Do you have your tickets for the jazz festival yet?' They talked like we were going forward. Keep it going forward."

- Possibly the loveliest gesture of all is recall. The person who can, in an non-obsequious manner, invoke or repeat a witticism or keen comment that his interlocutor made seven years ago is a friend forever. The person who remembers—even though you told him five weeks ago—that today is the day your loved one is being shipped overseas, or is being given an important medical diagnosis, is a person who is a joy to have around.

## Bringing Japan Home

If you look at the various jobs I've held over the years—I've been a summer camp counselor, a casting assistant, a Realtor's assistant, a headwaiter, a film production manager—one thing becomes clear: I am someone who *longs* to be given a blue blazer and a clipboard. At my core, the descriptors *slight busybody* and *good with details* seem to swirl in a tidal basin of efficiency—spilling out into a sluice gate labeled "effusive homosexual." It's only my mountainous ignorance of matters automotive that has kept me from manning the desk at a Hertz or Avis outpost; in my fantasy rental check-in, while the customer and I are walking around the vehicle looking for scratches and dings, we hold hands and discuss our mutual love for Emma Thompson.

Thus I'm hoping that you'll see a natural progression to things when I tell you that I volunteer as a kind of tour guide for foreigners who are visiting New York City. Alas, there's no blue blazer or clipboard, but both these items are implied. At times I can even feel the lanyard around my neck with the whistle.

The whole point of Big Apple Greeter, the organization I volunteer with, is to give visitors a chance to spend some time with a local. And this is indeed why I'm drawn to Big Apple—having traveled to foreign countries where the only locals I talked to were waiters or railroad employees, I know what it's like to think that all of a country's natives are surly, mustachioed character actors who find their current employment far beneath their dignity.

Like most of the foreigners who get in touch with Big Apple for visits, I'd read about it on an online travel site. A free public service started in 1992, Big Apple has about three hundred volunteer greeters and about thirty volunteers who work in the dot-org's offices.

As a prospective greeter, you fill out an application stating what neighborhoods in New York City you know well. A subsequent in-person interview downtown is brief and chatty; if successful, it is followed by a three-hour-long orientation with ten or so other greeters. You are repeatedly told (at my orientation, five times) that, for legal and financial reasons, you are not, not, *not* allowed to call yourself a tour guide—you're a greeter—and you do not give tours, you go on "visits." All this feels a bit like you're a prostitute who's trying to convince herself that her degree in social work was not in vain. But the Big Apple people are friendly and fun, and once you've taken the orientation, they send you a weekly e-mail listing of all the people looking for greeters, along with their dates, interests, nationalities, and lodging details.

Once I'd gotten over my disappointment that Big Apple does not provide its greeters with leis—the New York City lei, I'd decided, should be a chunky, amber-colored wreath that, on closer inspection, reveals itself to be Percocet vials—I devised a tour and thought about what New York lore I wanted to impart to my visitors.

The tour, sorry, *visit* itself was fairly easy to come up with: If you canvas the fourteen blocks around my office, located on Broadway near New York University, you find a fairly juicy sampling of architecture and design, starting with a far-off view of the Woolworth Building; then New York's only Louis Sullivan–designed building; a groovy, high-end condominium designed by the same people who did the Bird's Nest Olympic stadium in Beijing; a former restaurant supply store on the Bowery that now houses Patricia Field, the costume designer for *Sex and the City*; and ending with the slightly weird, Rem Koolhaas–designed Prada store, which used to have "ass-cams" (waist-directed cameras and monitors in the dressing rooms, for butt inspection).

My office is located at the nexus of several different neighborhoods—and crisscrossing between the areas of Soho, Noho, and NoLita is at times confusing for my visitors. As we walked across busy Houston Street, I explained to one German couple in their early thirties that Soho is an abbreviation of *so*uth of *Ho*uston. Pointing in front of us, I said, "That's Soho." Then pointing behind us, I added, "And that's Noho." A quizzical expression came over the husband's bearded, thoughtful visage and he asked, "So where are we now?"

"We're right on Ho itself."

He looked at the street slightly suspiciously and asked, "This…is Ho?"

"It would be impossible to be Ho-ier."

And for those who manage to remain unrattled by this, there are several fine downtown buildings at which I gaze, a bit emotionally, and note that "the World Trade Center was framed right between those two." Nothing throws the lightheartedness of a Manhattan afternoon into relief quite so handily as a stop at the Tora Bora Caves.

When I was starting out, it took longer for me to decide what, precisely, I wanted to share with these visitors about my city. I thought back to when I first moved to New York, and tried to remember what behavior I witnessed in New York that struck me as odd.

Gradually, three items emerged as standouts. First, New Yorkers are in the habit of starting up conversations with strangers at the least provocation, or none. This can happen anywhere, including on the street and in small, contained spaces. Second, New Yorkers have no trouble asking you how many square feet your house or apartment is, and how much you paid or pay for it. Third, New Yorkers cut in line and steal cabs.

"That's happened a lot already," one of my charges—a hearty British woman in her twenties—told me when I broached the topic of New Yorkers' gabbiness with her. She added, "You don't know whether to indulge them or not. They might be crazy."

"Probably the best policy, if you don't want to engage with them," I counseled her, "is to say something mild and then move along. Especially if there's a strong liquor smell."

"That might be the real offense—the smelling, not the talking," she said.

"Yes," I agreed. "And in combination: deadly."

When I explained New Yorkers' chatty tendencies to an older Australian couple, the husband nodded knowingly and, pointing to his tiny, cherubic wife, said, "They're always drawn to her."

Looking at the wife consolingly while I secretly surveilled her straw-brimmed hat and pink T-shirt, I said to her, "You look very friendly."

"They know that I'm one of them."

The topic of New Yorkers' interest in real estate candor is a much more baffling one for foreigners. "Talking about money like that would be absolutely taboo in Holland. Absolutely taboo," one Dutch woman, traveling with her college-aged daughter, told me. I told another Dutch woman—this one a smiley schoolteacher in her thirties traveling with her boyfriend—that New Yorkers sometimes ask how much rent you pay. I added, "When I first moved to New York, I was slightly flabbergasted by this."

"Flabberblasted because they were friends, or strangers?"

"Either. Would people ask that in Holland?"

"No, we don't talk about money."

"So if a New Yorker asks you, how will you respond?"

She thought a moment, and replied, "'I have a lovely garden. It will make you forget about money.'"

"That's good," I offered. "Now, what if you wanted to ask *them* how much they paid for rent?"

"I don't think I would."

"But say for some reason you had to. How would you ask?"

"'Are you happy with your apartment?'"

"That sounds like you're asking if it gets enough light."

"Yes. Okay." She looked at her boyfriend for guidance; he offered none. She tried again. "'Would you say that you had a good deal?'" She smiled a diplomat's smile and asked me, "How was that? Also, do I know this person well?"

"No. He's a total stranger."

She nodded and reiterated, "'Would you say you had a good deal?'"

"Pretty good," I said. "But New Yorkers are sometimes even more direct."

"I've seen on television shows where people write down numbers on a piece of paper and then pass it to the other person and ask if the number is 'comfortable' for them. Maybe I would do this? Write a number on a piece of paper and ask if the person is comfortable."

So far, the headiest reaction to being told that you might be asked how much your home costs came from the visitor in the straw hat. She told me, "They do it to see if you're in the same price range as them. To know whether or not they want to be friends with you."

"That's very dark," I told her.

"But this is how it is for some people."

That New Yorkers cut in lines and steal cabs is not, on the whole, news to foreigners, many of whom face such chicanery in their own countries. But what *did* strike them as interesting was my assertion that if they ever need a cab, they will need to be willing to steal one from someone else. A German woman who was visiting her daughter in New York responded: "Oh, so it is a game of dirty poker that you play!"

To wit, it is my belief that if indeed you are in great need of a cab—you're late for an appointment, or it is raining, or it is two in the morning and you are standing on a dicey part of Flatbush—then it is permissible to walk upstream of another party that is also hailing a cab, as long as you walk far enough upstream that that party cannot see you. Well, at least not glare at you.

"But they might walk up there and see you!" the German woman told me.

"Yes," I said. "But the trained assassin is both methodical and efficient."

## Local Product

A slight awkwardness permeates many of these outings. First, because I am giving a tour but I am not giving a tour, and second because, whatever it is that I *am* doing, I can do it for as long or as little time as I want to. (My orientation leader had explained that most visits last two to three hours, but Big Apple doesn't check in on you, so you are running your own show.) So sometimes, in order to deflate my visitors' possible fear of days-long entrapment, I will try to give these folks a kind of road map. I'll say, "We'll be walking around Noho for about twenty minutes, and then around Soho for about forty minutes, and then we can decide if we want to go on to China-town or the West Village for another half hour or so." I'm someone who loves to know what the running time of a theatrical event will be, particularly if it is a one-person show or if I will be looking at a leotard. Knowing this information gives me scope and dimension; it allows my bowels to exhale relievedly like a manta ray settling on the ocean floor.

I will also sometimes under-represent how many tours I've given—I'll say, "You're only my fourth tour"— because I want the walk to feel like mutual discovery rather than sitting in an un-air-conditioned church basement for an annual slide show called "Telephone Poles I Have Known." Also, I want to lower their expectations of my professionalism so that any actual spark of merit seems like a forest fire. It's like when the construction of Radio City Music Hall was finished and they put nitrous oxide in the ventilating system for opening night. Some things just need a little magic, a little boost.

Other than my own occasional lapse—I twice have told visitors about lavishing attention on previous visitors, and then felt guilty when I spent only an hour or so with these newer folks—I've seen only good manners, not bad, on my tours. All of these folks have thanked me for my time, some have given me books about their cities or villages; many want to take pictures with me. A tea towel emblazoned with scenes of County Cork entered my life at a particularly apt, Irish-linen-less time; two Brazilian girls once foisted banana pudding on me. Occasionally people try to give me money, whereupon I launch into a spritz of glib refusal and chittering that I would seem to have patterned on my Tokyo mentor, J.J.

Tours with those traveling alone are more intense than with couples or trios. Indeed, the one friendship

I've made from this experience is with a hipster dentist from Buenos Aires with whom, during the course of his ten days in the States, I went out for lunch twice, and to a gospel service in Harlem. I knew he and I were going to become friends when he told me, "Tour guides in the United States always tell you how much buildings cost. This is very interesting to them."

I also enjoyed spending time with the handsome Dutch epidemiologist (specialty: leprosy). After lunch and a four-hour tour, we made plans to get together for a beer the following afternoon. But when I hugged him good-bye outside the building where my office is, I thought, Oh, I've given him the wrong impression. Indeed, in a subsequent e-mail, the flight that he was supposed to take the following evening at nine was now mysteriously at five, precluding a beer.

I'll call a third solo traveler—a boyish gentleman in his thirties from Jordan—Talal. When I met Talal in front of his hotel as we'd planned, we said hello and introduced ourselves to each other. Then he said, "I have a gift for you."

"Oh, that's sweet. You didn't have to do that."

"Are you married?"

"No."

"Do you have a girl?"

"No."

"Because I brought some local product for her. Something from Jordan."

Given that this exchange was conducted within thirty seconds of meeting Talal, and given that Talal was from a Muslim country, I uncharacteristically refrained from pointing out that I have a boyfriend. My reluctance stemmed not from a sense of decorum—on this topic, manners be damned. Nor did this reluctance stem from a desire to slyly point out Talal's own social maladroitness to him. Rather, I like to feel that I am in control of this revelation and its timing.

What made the four hours I spent with Talal particularly piquant was that we witnessed examples of or variants on all three varieties of the New York City brutalities I told him about. After walking around for a couple of hours, we decided to get some lunch in Chinatown. Entering one of my favorite restaurants on Mott Street, thinking we might get some soup dumplings, we waited in line for five minutes but decided to leave when three people cut in line in front of us (see aforementioned, People in NYC Will Cut in Lines). Then we walked over to a huge dim sum palace, where we sat at a large round, communal table populated by a Chinese family of three and a middle-aged, round-eye couple.

"I must tell you something," Talal said to me after I'd wrangled some shrimp dumplings off a cart. "Sixty percent of Jordanians are Palestinian. I am Palestinian."

I nodded my head in interest. "You're probably smart to be discreet about that," I said, speaking in a slightly hushed voice.

The middle-aged Caucasian woman, sitting three chairs away from us, said, "Did I hear you say you're from Palestine?" (see aforementioned, People in NYC Will Start Talking to You for No Reason), whereupon she and her husband—both Jewish, and both very politically open-minded—proceeded to have a surprisingly calm conversation with Talal about the West Bank. During which the wife managed to work in the information that she and her husband pay twenty-eight hundred dollars for their three-bedroom in Murray Hill. (People in New York Are Obsessed with Real Estate.)

## Eff Declension

Over the course of the visits I've conducted—I've now given thirty-nine—I've noticed two developments. One is that the impulse to guide and assist is sometimes without bounds: I am now compelled to get all guide-y with random foreigners I see on the street. This might be as brief as the thirty-second-long exchange I had with a hearty, grandfatherly-looking man photographing the Louis Sullivan building.

Me: Is that building in your guidebook?

Him: No.

Me: Because that was designed by Louis Sullivan, the father of the skyscraper, who was Frank Lloyd Wright's mentor.

Him: I did not know.

Me: You have good taste!

Him (Awkward smile, staring at ground): My wife is thinking this also.

Or it might take the form of an actual tour. A young, French student of architecture who was stumbling around the NYU area one morning was thrilled to have me show him both a Thom Mayne building and, just a few blocks away, a Herzog & de Meuron building; a fiftyish Croatian woman who asked me for directions was slightly less indulgent of my pedagogy as I accompanied her for twenty-five minutes or so, pointing out items of interest along the way. ("Yes, I know that. The Woolworth Building is very famous," she let me know at one point. Our subsequent parting did not fill her with mourning.)

I've also taken to adding to my small menu of New Yorky behavior some New Yorky turns of phrase that might confuse the uninitiated foreigner. *Fuhgeddaboudit* and *schlepp* get the most airtime, but I have also covered *goombah, youse,* and, once, *you got lot shit whichoo.* An Englishman who witnessed an aggrieved commercial transaction on the sidewalk one day asked me what is meant by the phrase *a freakin' dolla.* So I add that to my repertoire sometimes, too. "It's an intensifier," I told one hip Dutch woman in her twenties. "It has some of the power of 'effing' but it's an 'effing' you could say in front of your mother and her best friend." The Dutch woman blinked at me and asked, "But why would I?"

I've also gotten into the habit of bringing foreigners to a touristy store on Bleecker Street that proudly displays, hanging on its door that opens onto the sidewalk, T-shirts emblazoned with New Yorkisms such as FUCK YOU YOU FUCKING FUCK and DO I LOOK LIKE A FUCKING PEOPLE PERSON?

"This is a bit of local charm," I'll usually tell my visitors; or if their English is good, I'll say, "Here's a little hello from our local chamber of commerce." Occasionally the visitors are unimpressed—one Danish graduate student (habituated to Denmark's tolerance for profanity) told me she was surprised to hear on American radio a heavily bleeped version of a song "by the rapper Jay Zed." But most people's initial reactions to the shirts involve eye widening or lip pursing.

Both these facial gestures were the hallmark of two zaftig English women in their forties—friends since college—to whom I showed the shirts one warm weekday afternoon.

"Oh, my," Geraldine, the more talkative of the two, said.

"To give you a bit of context: New Yorkers swear a lot. Clearly," I said. "Also, on these shores the playwright David Mamet is considered very talented."

"It's from a David Mamet play, that?" Geraldine asked, pointing to the f-you-you-f-f garment.

"No, it's from the movie *Blue Velvet*," I said. "But in general the interest in fuck declension is Mamet-derived."

The phrase *fuck declension* hung in the air like a particularly eggy blast of methane.

"Ooh. My son would like that one." Sylvia redirected our energies, pointing to a T-shirt bearing the words FUCK MILK. GOT POT? "But I couldn't buy it for him."

"I could," Geraldine suggested rhetorically.

Sylvia answered, "Yes, you could. But if *I* did, end of story. 'Mother Rendered Suddenly Powerless.'"

When I posited my opinion that New Yorkers engage in a high incidence of profanity, one South African gentleman—ruddy, heavyset, rheumy-eyed—told me, "The Irish swear the most of any nationality. They have no other adjectives!" Two tours later, I repeated this comment to a young man from Belfast, who lamented, "Well, ye can't really blame us now, can ye?"

"You mean, because of the potato famine and the bad weather and the poverty and everything?" I asked.

"Fecking 'ell—you make us sound like we live in a hole," he said.

"I'm sorry."

"You needn't apologize. I'm just pointin' out yer own shortcomin's."

## Portrait

Sometimes I wonder what kind of portrait of my city I've ended up painting for my new friends. Ultimately, I hope my guidance and my calm will somehow mitigate the fact that I am, in the main, pointing out stereotypes and trying to make these stereotypes more understandable or possibly lovable. One of my charges asked me, "Do New Yorkers realize they're being rude when they ask how much rent you pay?" Which made me think. "No. They're trying to commiserate with you," I offered. "Unless you have a particularly sweet deal, in which case they want to kill you." But either way, it's not rude. It's part of the mores of here.

Interactions like these make me think that maybe I *am* on a visit rather than a tour. Two people visit together; one visits another; a foreigner or out-of-towner visits my city. A tour is something one gets *taken* on. The difference may seem semantic. But it just starts out semantic. Once you start swapping thoughts about the behavior of your fellow citizens, then you've moved beyond the confines of an ambulatory travelogue.

On at least one occasion, after saying good-bye to visitors and watching them walk down Broadway and slowly fade into the crowd, I think of the sum total of what I've said to these people, and of the image of my city that I've given them. My hunch is that while, on the good side, I've painted a picture that is arty, curious, fast-paced, and cosmopolitan, it's also one that celebrates cutting in line and giving voice to questions that some might think better suppressed.

But this is how it should be, no? In Japan, they teach

you how to be modest by using chopsticks correctly and by not leaving scuff marks on the tatami, and in New York we teach you how to be rude by stealing cabs and asking intrusive questions about real estate—because that's all part of the local etiquette. To omit this from our teachings would be, well, bad manners.

If the image of New York I've conjured up for my visitors is more hard-edged than I might want it, it is nevertheless entirely up to its recipient to refute or further substantiate same. That I'm offering this picture in the first place is half this bargain's charm. I'm a snapshot. And for this, I make no apologies.

## Hail Caesar

Toward the end of my interview with Miss Manners in the lobby of my DC hotel, I mentioned that I'd been teaching foreigners how to steal a cab.

"I can never get a cab in New York," she told me. "How do you get the cab to stop?"

"They're not seeing you?"

"Yes. Or something. I think they can tell who's not a New Yorker."

"Are you standing out far enough in the street? You've got to be out in the traffic."

"Out in the traffic, but not run over."

"Right," I said. "But you've got to be a little brazen.

And the rule for stealing a cab is that you've got to walk at least a block upstream."

"So people don't see you."

"Yes."

She nodded, a gestural *I see.*

Some ten minutes later, interview concluded, I asked Miss Manners if I could call her a cab, but she said she was just going to get one out on the street. "Let me walk you out," I offered. "I want to show you my hailing technique."

We walked some twenty yards to the end of the street, where I stuck my arm out into the traffic.

Was there, about fifty yards downstream of us, a harried-looking businesswoman also trying to hail a cab? Was there a frantic husband holding the hand of his pregnant wife whose water had just broken, and whose energetic flaggings directed at the oncoming traffic were like an evening of Twyla Tharp titled *Medical Emergency*?

My lips are sealed.

Roughly twelve seconds after I'd stepped off the curb and extended my arm, a cab materialized.

"Wow," Miss Manners said. "You really *do* have a technique."

## The Face of Battle

In his book *The Face of Battle*, British military historian John Keegan wonders why, when faced with the horrors of war, more soldiers don't flee. He concludes that these brave souls don't remain steadfast out of a sense of duty or patriotism, but rather so as not to be the least noble person in their company or peer group. Our need to preserve our dignity, if not our strong desire to escape humiliation, serves as a kind of beacon. "Even under the most extreme and appalling conditions," Randy Cohen writes in *The Good, the Bad and the Difference: How to Tell Right from Wrong in Everyday Situations*, "most of us behave about as well as our neighbors."

I understand, and wholly sympathize with, this analysis.

It speaks volumes about what motivates humans.

And it depresses me to my very core.

Granted, the fact that most of us will maintain the semblance of good manners simply because we're being watched or because we fear criticism shouldn't, in one sense, matter: Whatever motivates us to get to Johnson's "fictitious benevolence" is fine. Better fictitious benevolence than no benevolence at all.

But in a larger sense—can't we do a little better? Is it naive to think that the physical expressing of benevolence might occasionally have a more stirring or palpable end product than mere fictitiousness?

I hope not.

## Why I Even Bother

I was walking around the East Village with a ruddy Frenchman and his twenty-two-year-old son. The tour had started off with a lot of long silences from the two men, but gradually the father warmed up and became quite a chatterbox. At one point he asked me, "So, we wonder why you are doing these tours? You are not paid."

"No, I'm not," I said, neatly dodging a chocolate-smeared candy wrapper on the sidewalk. "But I love getting out of the office in the afternoon. And it's fun to meet new people."

The Frenchman squinted his eyes determinedly, as if his eyelids might squeeze or juice some bit of insight from the surface of his eyes.

"But you are hoping also that the favor will be returned if you come to our country?"

"Not really," I confessed. "Plus, I already lost your e-mail address."

"So it's mostly for the experience."

"Yes." Mostly for the experience. That sounded about right.

But then something else occurred to me, too: "Also, I love hearing Germans say *fuhgeddaboudit*."

"Oh, yes? This is fun?"

"It's amazing," I told him. "It's like a documentary about umlauts."

*Acknowledgments*

A thousand thanks to George Kalogerakis. A thousand thanks to Jonathan Karp. A thousand thanks to David McCormick. A thousand thanks to Jess Taylor. A thousand thanks to editor Colin Shepherd.

Also: Cary Goldstein, Brian McLendon, Laura Jorstad, Pete Wells, Susan Morrison, Laura Marmor, Stuart Emmrich, Gail Morse, Rory Evans, Ryan Haney, Aimee Bell, Greg Villepique, Sandra Tsing Loh, Tareth Mitch, Jennifer Weisberg. Y'all are kind.

# Index

*About the Author*

HENRY ALFORD has written for *Vanity Fair*, and *The New York Times* for over a decade; he has also written for the *New Yorker*. His books include *How to Live*, about the wisdom of the elderly, and *Big Kiss*, which won a Thurber Prize. He is often heard on National Public Radio.

# ABOUT TWELVE

TWELVE

TWELVE was established in August 2005 with the objective of publishing no more than one book per month. We strive to publish the singular book, by authors who have a unique perspective and compelling authority. Works that explain our culture; that illuminate, inspire, provoke, and entertain. We seek to establish communities of conversation surrounding our books. Talented authors deserve attention not only from publishers, but from readers as well. To sell the book is only the beginning of our mission. To build avid audiences of readers who are enriched by these works—that is our ultimate purpose.

For more information about forthcoming TWELVE books, please go to www.twelvebooks.com.